SACRED
INVITATION

*Lenten Devotions Inspired by
the Book of Common Prayer*

Copyright © 2020 by The Foundry Publishing
The Foundry Publishing
PO Box 419527
Kansas City, MO 64141
thefoundrypublishing.com

978-0-8341-3917-6

Printed in the
United States of America

Cover and Interior Design: Arthur Cherry
Layout: Michael J. Williams

10 9 8 7 6 5 4 3 2 1

CONTENTS

INTRODUCTION

Some of us seem to wander aimlessly through our Christian journey, grateful for the grace of God but without a real sense of direction or purpose. On some level we all crave a sense of purpose that impacts our present reality, not merely our future in Christ, but it is often difficult to discern the voice of God amidst the chaos of life in this world.

The purpose of the season of Lent in the Christian calendar is to help us orient our lives toward the central celebration of the Christian faith: the resurrection from the dead of Jesus the Messiah. When we direct our hearts toward that event through the practice of Christian disciplines, the Spirit has the space to reorient our lives and to provide a deeply meaningful and eternally significant purpose to our daily lives. Writing to the Philippian church, Paul put it this way: "I want to know Christ—yes, to know the power of his resurrection and participation in his sufferings, becoming like him in his death, and so, somehow, attaining to the resurrection from the dead" (3:10–11). Paul's life was focused on the central reality of the resurrection of Jesus from the dead. Once that became a reality to him, nothing else mattered as much.

The purpose of this devotional is to prepare us for an appropriate celebration of and a sincere participation in the resurrection of Jesus from the dead. The season of Easter—the period of time between Easter Sunday and Pentecost—is so much more than just another religious observance. It is the recognition that the resurrection of Jesus changed everything. Through the death and resurrection of Jesus, new creation burst forth into human time and space. God's redeeming, restoring, healing intentions for us and for the world were unleashed. Only when Christ returns will the old pass away entirely and new creation be complete, but the work has begun. What God did for Jesus, God will also do for the entire cosmos. We—followers of the resurrected Christ—have a profound sense of purpose for our lives as we live toward new creation life even now.

We have written these devotional thoughts and guides for reflection with a single-minded focus: to prepare the church to grasp the life-changing reality of the life, death, and resurrection of Jesus. As we walk this journey through Lent, we may find our place in that grand story—but that takes focus. It requires that we become intentional about searching our lives and hearts. We must be honest and vulnerable, humbly allowing the Spirit to reveal both sin and the wounds that lead to destructive patterns. Forgiveness and healing await.

It is our hope that we will all hunger to know Christ, to know the power of his resurrection and participation in his sufferings. Perhaps our Easter celebration can have a richer and more significant texture to it as a result. So, we issue you this *Sacred Invitation* to gather with others and walk through this season together. And let's get ready to celebrate.

Jesse C Middendorf (JCM)
Stephanie Dyrness Lobdell (SDL)

ASH WEDNESDAY

AM Psalms: 32, 95, 143

PM Psalms: 102, 130

Jonah 3:1–4:11

Luke 18:9–14

Hebrews 12:1–14

The Pharisees often get a bum rap. For many of them, humility before God was as natural as breathing. With a deep love and respect for the Law as the revelation of the mind of God, the Pharisee was often one of the most devout, sensitive, and humble people around. But, as is the case with some Christians today, it is altogether possible to be immersed in your own righteousness. When we look with contempt at people who seem to be not as visibly religious as we feel ourselves to be, we fall into a dangerous trap.

The Pharisee in the parable of Jesus was not judged for being righteous. He was judged for being contemptuous. He looked down on those whom he judged as sinners. He even catalogued some of the assumptions he was making toward those sinners: "robbers, evildoers, adulterers" (Luke 18:11).

In contrast, the tax collector stood at a distance, beating his breast and pleading for mercy. He might well have been tempted to hold the Pharisee in contempt as one who paraded his righteousness. But the tax collector was not interested in comparisons. He was desperate for mercy.

The Old Testament Law made abundantly clear that those who broke the Law with malice and intent were to be dealt with immediately and harshly. Adulterers, murderers, and the like were to be executed. Other offenses required banishment from Israel. The sacrificial system was not for atonement for the high-handed sinner. It was for unintentional sins—the imperfections in the performance of right attitudes and actions in daily living. The people of Israel were taught to live with humility, with a deep reliance on the mercy and grace of God as it was demonstrated and administered through the many sacrificial offerings made for the nation and for individuals.

For Christians, our justification and redemption are provided by the suffering death and glorious resurrection of Jesus Christ. We are never to forget that grace is a free gift, neither deserved nor earned. And grace is given in such measure that we may be set free from the awful power and dominion of sin. But we continue to live with the limitations that come with being human in a broken world. Though our redemption is complete, it is not final. We are not yet glorified and living in the New Jerusalem.

The season of Lent is valuable to us because of our human limitations and the free grace that Christ offers us from the cross. In this season we rehearse a way of living that should characterize our lives all year long. We are reminded of our frailty. We are humbly brought to face our vulnerability and imperfections as we encounter the brokenness and sin around us. This season gives us structure for intentionally seeking to live with humility, contrition, confession, and trust as we prepare to confront the brokenness with mercy, compassion, and healing grace.

We invite you to join us and those around you on this journey. Lean in and live!

—JCM

REFLECTION & PRACTICE

The prayer of the Pharisee seems to indicate that he was enslaved by the lie that, because he was not a "sinner" in a visible and dramatic way, he was less in need of mercy from God. His contemptuous prayer reveals spiritual pride over gratitude. What attitudes or behaviors might reveal a contemptuous, prideful spirit in ourselves? What might that prideful posture manifest in our relationships?

The tax collector is under no illusions concerning his righteousness. He knows himself to be in desperate need of mercy. How might attentiveness to our own sinful patterns and need for grace free us from the subtle allure of comparative righteousness?

We have been set free from the chains of sin and death by the work of Christ, yet we live in a world not yet restored and healed. Does the reality of the power of sin still at work in the world condemn us to persist in sinful patterns? Why or why not?

During Lent, we are challenged to "rehearse a way of living." We choose humility over pride, confession over hiding behind a façade of false perfection. What might it look like for you to intentionally practice the disciplines of humility and confession?

PRAYER

Lord, we confess that we have stood before you, confident in our own righteousness. We have used comparison as the measure and failed to recognize the sins of pride and contempt in our own hearts. Give us the courage to lay ourselves bare before you and allow the Spirit to uncover the sinful patterns in us. As we begin this Lenten journey once again, empower us to practice humility and confession, that we might experience the wonder of your grace and forgiveness once again.

THURSDAY

AM Psalm: 37:1–18

PM Psalm: 37:19–42

Deuteronomy 7:6–11

John 1:29–34

Titus 1:1–16

One of the great temptations of contemporary Christianity is to insist on instant gratification, immediate results, or step-by-step approaches to an encounter with God. The value of a *season* of Lent is the necessity of a determined and consistent endeavor to prepare our hearts for such an encounter. In the scriptures for today we are reminded that we must be patient with the long, slow, sometimes imperceptible movement of God on our behalf.

Psalm 37 is a call to perseverance: "Be still before the LORD and wait patiently for him; do not fret when people succeed in their ways, when they carry out their wicked schemes" (v. 7).

Titus is left on the island of Crete, where he is to establish the new and developing church of Jesus Christ. But the task is hard. The people are obstinate and resistant to the message. It is discouraging enough to cause him to consider abandoning the project. But Paul is insistent: *Stay with it. This is why I left you there. It will be difficult, but persevere.* (See Titus 1:8–9.)

When John baptizes Jesus, he witnesses the Holy Spirit descend "and remain" on Jesus (1:32). But the mission of the Messiah is not immediately complete. John, in spite of what he witnessed at the baptism, will yet experience imprisonment, uncertainty, and martyrdom.

Lent is a season of preparation. We know the end of the story, but in this season, as we prepare for the celebration of the resurrection, we must remind ourselves that the journey is neither quick nor easy. During these forty days (not counting Sundays), you are invited and encouraged to read the daily scriptures, to examine your own heart and life choices, and to open yourself to the probing and challenging presence of the Holy Spirit.

For those for whom the observance of Lent is a new experience, this is a season within the Christian year that is built around the life and mission of Jesus. It begins with Advent—a celebration of Jesus coming to earth as an infant as well as the anticipation of his coming again one day. It includes the celebration of Easter, Pentecost, and the work of the church of Jesus Christ in God's mission to prepare the world for the return of Jesus. The Christian year provides a means of orienting the life of the church—and the life of each of us as followers of Jesus—around the significant events and teachings of Jesus.

During Lent we prepare our hearts to embrace the meaning of the suffering death and resurrection of Jesus on our behalf. Many choose to lay aside some legitimate things or practices for the season in order to discipline our minds and hearts to focus more clearly on Jesus and his teachings.

Enter into this season with a humble spirit, an open mind, and a hungry heart. Ask the Spirit to probe your heart and mind, to reveal places of needed growth and surrender. Let the long, slow work of the Spirit lead you deeper into relationship with Jesus and his people.

—JCM

REFLECTION & PRACTICE

01 Think of a time you were in a season of waiting. What emotions did you experience? How did the process of waiting shape you over time?

02 While we would often prefer the work of God to be wrought in us instantly, God sometimes chooses to teach and shape us over time. We are transformed as we submit in trusting obedience. Consider past seasons of change. Looking back, how can you more clearly identify the work of God that might have been unclear or hidden from you at the time?

03 Stillness does not indicate absence. Difficulty does not indicate unfaithfulness. Suffering does not indicate we are on the wrong path. How does culture's avoidance of pain and discomfort as well as the idolatry of happiness hinder us from persisting in faithfulness on the often difficult road of discipleship?

04 Lent is not about giving up sweets, coffee, or social media. It is about clearing space in our hearts and minds to allow us to focus on following Jesus. Addictions (like, perhaps, to sweets or coffee) may be revealed. Toxic habits (like, for instance, the way we use social media) might make themselves known. But God in God's mercy only illuminates wounds the Spirit is ready and willing to heal.
   - What might it look like to create space in your heart and mind this Lenten season?
   - What might be the implications of this space-making for your daily habits and patterns?

PRAYER

Lord, we confess our impatience of heart and our often anemic devotion to transformative spiritual disciplines. In our hectic and harried state, we fail to hear your invitation to make space in our lives for your work. Forgive us our restlessness and cultivate within us an unhurried spirit that remains attentive to you even in seasons of stillness. Teach us the discipline of persistent trust.

FRIDAY

AM Psalms: 31, 95

PM Psalm: 35

Deuteronomy 7:12–16

John 1:35–42

Titus 2:1–15

One of the objectives of the Lenten season is to achieve greater intimacy with Jesus. In the early church, the season of Lent was the period of preparation for baptism for those who had come to know Jesus. Typically baptisms were held on Easter Sunday, and those who were to be baptized were nurtured, taught, and discipled in anticipation of their joining the community of believers.

Lent is a good time for us to cultivate our own intimacy with Jesus. How helpful this can be when done in community, joining with others in preparing our hearts for the Easter celebration.

John 1:35–42 recounts how Andrew and Peter become followers of Jesus—his earliest disciples. They follow him, going to where he is staying, perhaps participating in an evening meal with him, possibly even spending the night with him. One of the primary responsibilities for us is to develop an intimate relationship with Jesus—which is not a matter of head knowledge. It is *relationship*. It is deeply investing in getting to know Jesus as we open ourselves to the presence of his Spirit, guided by the Word.

But reading the letter to Titus can be overwhelming. Planting and nurturing the church in Crete is not an easy matter. The culture is crude and in constant agitation. As part of the Roman Empire, it is subject to, among other things, the norms of slavery, the subjugation of women, and the abuse of alcohol. Sexual immorality is rampant, and hopelessness is widespread.

Knowing and following Jesus, according to Paul, is the only adequate antidote to such a broken world. Almost every admonition given to Titus underscores the necessity of living counter-culturally. At a profound and almost inexpressible level, Paul is utterly convinced that the hope for the world is in knowing and following Jesus Christ. Knowing Jesus, living as Jesus taught us to live, living in communion with those of like mind, is paramount—but it is not for their own sake. Everyone, even slaves, is to live in such a way as to demonstrate the integrity that following Jesus produces: "to show that they can be fully trusted, so that in every way they will make the teaching about God our Savior attractive" (Titus 2:10). This train of thought is not an embrace of slavery as an acceptable social and economic reality. It is meant to open the door for the gospel to begin to unravel all the bondage, brokenness, and evil that lurks in the culture of Crete.

When two of John the Baptist's followers spend the day with Jesus, everything in their lives changes. One of them, Andrew, immediately finds his brother, Simon, and invites him to follow Jesus too. Knowing Jesus changes everything.

During this season of preparation, get to know Jesus. Open yourself up to him, to the Word, and to the community of faith as you walk toward Easter. If you really hunger to help unravel the brokenness in the culture around you, get to know Jesus at a deeper level than you have known him up to now. The change in you will begin to change everything around you. Dig in!

—JCM

REFLECTION & PRACTICE

01 Jesus's response to the first disciples following after him is not to deliver a theological treatise or even a sermon. Rather, he simply invites them to "come and see" (John 1:39). It is an invitation to bear witness to what God is doing in their midst.

- How has God invited you to bear witness to God's work in the world? How did that experience transform you?
- How might we extend Jesus's invitation to others who do not yet know him, that they might "come and see" what God is doing?

02 Like the congregation in Crete, we too live in a culture marked by immorality, both in personal lifestyle choices and also in systemic social and economic abuses. The latter often feel beyond our control, so we focus our attention almost exclusively on personal piety. How might devoting ourselves to knowing and loving Jesus more deeply challenge us to confront both personal sin in our lives and also systemic sin in the world around us?

03 The power of the gospel unleashed can unravel bondage and bind up wounds in our hearts and in the world.

- How have you experienced the freedom and healing of the gospel?
- What might it look like to be an agent of that freedom and healing in your immediate context?

PRAYER

Lord, you have invited us to know you deeply. We confess that we have often settled for knowing you as an acquaintance. We have contented ourselves with familiarity. We long for freedom and healing, both in ourselves and in the world, yet we resist transformative intimacy. Awaken our sleepy spirits and quiet our fears, that we might courageously open our lives to you fully in order to know you well and follow you faithfully.

SATURDAY

AM Psalms: 30, 32

PM Psalms: 42, 43

Deuteronomy 7:17–26

John 1:43–51

Titus 3:1–15

"Can anything good come from . . . ?" You name the place, or the people, or the church, or the circumstance. We so easily draw our judgments and conclusions, most often because of our prejudices, whether conscious or unconscious.

Perhaps as fully as any passage in the Gospels, the response of Nathanael to Philip's invitation to meet Jesus reveals the challenge of the incarnation of the Son of God. Kings and Messiahs don't come from Nazareth, an insignificant village in the hills of Galilee, far from the city of Jerusalem! And developing the church in Crete (see the letter to Titus) is hard because, well, *those* people!

In painful self-awareness, most of us must acknowledge that there are some people, places, groups, lifestyles—even some religions—about which we form harsh, critical, and judgmental opinions and attitudes. It is so obvious on social media, where many vent their inner anger toward "those people," whoever they may be, whatever the issue of the moment. But for those deeply hungering to follow Christ and become more like him, there is a challenge presented to us: The more we study his life, and the more we desire to reflect his character, the more we find that there was no limit to where his love would reach.

If you read Deuteronomy for today, you might be tempted to believe that God is callously determined to destroy those whom God thinks deserve destruction. While we review the history of the people of God as they make their way into the promised land, we dare not forget that the God about whom we read is not most fully revealed in the Old Testament story. The full and final revelation of God is Jesus! God is like Jesus! God has always been like Jesus. God *will* always be like Jesus! And Jesus reaches out to all humanity—even those we resist or detest—in redeeming love.

Our task as followers of Jesus is to guard our hearts from the disease of sinful self-interest—which is why we are often threatened by people who are not like us, whose life experiences and values are so utterly unlike ours. But we dare not consign other human beings into categories of acceptable or unacceptable based on our judgments of them. That does not mean we ignore the destructiveness of sin, or the danger of indulging in harmful behavior and habits. It does mean we extend love and acceptance to everyone. It means we engage in restoration and recovery for broken people. It means we address human need—whatever its manifestation— with holy love and tangible, personal, sacrificial relationships. We feed the hungry, clothe the naked, and visit the sick and imprisoned because that man from Nazareth said we should (see Matthew 25:31–46)!

Don't let your Lenten journey be too safe. Let Jesus challenge your preconceptions and reveal your prejudices. Let him call you out and send you into the fray, your heart pounding and your mind whirling. It may be the most adventurous journey you have ever taken.

—JCM

REFLECTION & PRACTICE

01 Nathanael is so bound up in his prejudice that he is unable to imagine God working in and through Nazareth and its people.
- What types of prejudices misshape our thinking and limit our imaginations for how God might work?
- What might happen if we asked God to unveil our unconscious biases and convict our spirits of our prejudices?

02 It is easy to justify negative attitudes toward certain people or people groups when we don't like or agree with their choices or beliefs.
- What might happen if we suspended judgment and practiced empathy and humble listening instead?
- How might practicing empathy and humility transform us and, perhaps, even transform the experience of the ones against whom we hold negative attitudes?

03 In Titus, Paul reminds the congregation of Crete that they were once "foolish, disobedient, deceived and enslaved by all kinds of passions and pleasures" (3:3), and God saved them not because of their righteousness but because of God's mercy, rooted in God's kindness and love.
- From what has God delivered you? What is God continuing to heal in you? Addiction, pride, selfishness, anger?
- How might practicing gratitude for God's deliverance in our lives enable us to demonstrate kindness and gentleness to others?

PRAYER

Lord, we like to imagine ourselves as neutral and free of unconscious bias, but in humility we confess that our hearts are plagued with prejudice. Instead of practicing empathy and humble listening to those different from us, we often stand apart in critique and condemnation. How easily we forget that from which you have delivered us. How quickly we forget that we too are being healed and restored in the image of Jesus. With holy trepidation, we invite your Spirit to convict our biases, forgive us our blindness, and heal our vision, that we might see all your children as beloved and made in your image.

FIRST SUNDAY

IN LENT

AM Psalms: 63, 98

PM Psalm: 103

Deuteronomy 8:1–10

Mark 2:18–22

1 Corinthians 1:17–31

For many who observe the Lenten season it is a matter of personal discipline and spiritual preparation to select some form of self-denial or fasting during the season. Fasting is one of the practices of the people of God in both the Old and New Testaments. Fasting is intended to focus our attention as we humble ourselves before God, forgoing a legitimate practice or a chosen food item.

Jesus fasted during the forty days in the wilderness when he was tempted by Satan to choose alternative methods to fulfill his redemptive mission. The believers in Antioch, while worshiping the Lord and fasting, heard the Holy Spirit direct them to commission Paul and Barnabas for their first missionary journey (Acts 13:1–3).

The importance of fasting, especially in times of great need, is demonstrated by the followers of John the Baptist and the Pharisees. In the passage from Mark's Gospel for today, people come to Jesus to ask why, since the disciples of John and the Pharisees are fasting, Jesus's disciples are not fasting. Jesus certainly does not diminish the importance of fasting, but he does indicate the appropriate reasons to fast. In doing so, he also makes it clear that our fasting is not an end in itself. Fasting is a means of focusing our attention in prayer toward the cultivation of a deeper and more profound communication with God. Failing to fast is not a sin. In fact, since "the bridegroom"—Jesus himself—is near, there is no immediate need to fast (Mark 2:19).

I once heard the late Dr. Dennis Kinlaw, an eminent Old Testament scholar, say that for the ancient Hebrew people, it was as inappropriate to fast on a feast day as it was to feast on a fast day. Jesus makes it clear that fasting is intended to help us have a more intimate, focused relationship with God—a ritual made unnecessary by God's very presence standing before them in Jesus.

An interesting tradition in Lenten observance is lifting the fast on Sundays when believers gather in worship. We are celebrating the lordship of Jesus, our redemption from guilt and condemnation, and our deliverance from the power of sin—all of which is made possible by Jesus's suffering death and resurrection.

I do hope you are willing to engage in some substantive means of self-denial or fasting during Lent. It should not be frivolous or showy. It is not to impress God or others. It is a means of denying ourselves in order to focus our hunger—our desire—into knowing Jesus better. That is one good reason for the observance of Lent. Set aside the routine. Focus your attention on Jesus. Examine your heart. Probe your life and practices. Let the fresh wind of the Holy Spirit lead you deeper into the likeness of Jesus.

On this day, the first Sunday of Lent, set a pattern for the following Lenten Sundays. Sing out loud. Worship the Source of your redemption. Set aside the fasting and self-denial for this day and bask in the abundant love of God as revealed in the gift of the Son. This is the Lord's day! Celebrate Jesus!

—JCM

REFLECTION & PRACTICE

01 Both fasting and feasting are spiritual disciplines in that they have the potential to draw our hearts and minds to God in trusting obedience.
- In what ways might feasting draw us into a deeper awareness of God's presence and work in and around us?
- What might it look like to intentionally practice feasting these Sundays of Lent?

02 When our hearts are not fixed on God, fasting can easily morph into a form of self-abuse by which we may hope to manipulate God. Feasting can devolve into self-indulgence and a sense of entitlement.
- How can we cultivate self-awareness and spiritual sensitivity to our motives?
- What role might the body of Christ play in practicing these spiritual disciplines well?

03 Because of the extended nature of fasting, it is primarily practiced alone. Feasting, on the other hand, is truly a collective discipline. In our celebratory gathering, we are reminded that Christ is in our midst.
- With whom might you practice the discipline of feasting this year?
- How might you extend the table to welcome those who might be on the fringe of the community?

PRAYER

Lord, on this day of rest we give thanks for your provision. As we gather with our sisters and brothers of the faith, we are reminded of your presence in and among us. As we journey toward the cross with you once again this year, we pause to celebrate in trust. You have come; you will come again. You were raised to new life; so too shall we be raised. In faithful hope, we worship you today among the corporate gathering of our fellow believers. Bless our feasting and celebration, and may the memory of our joy today carry us through the upcoming week of self-denial.

MONDAY

AM Psalms: 41, 52

PM Psalm: 44

Deuteronomy 8:11–18

John 2:1–12

Hebrews 2:11–18

Weddings sometimes produce memorable moments that last a lifetime. Some of them are humorous. Some are poignant. Some are stunning in their depth of meaning. Whatever the case, those who may have been present at a wedding—and who are privileged to celebrate anniversaries with the couple many years later—often engage in conversations that begin, "Do you remember . . . ?"

I have often wondered what the anniversary conversations may have been like for the couple whose wedding Jesus attended in Cana of Galilee. Did the couple even know what happened? Was it a pleasant surprise to have been complimented by the "master of the banquet" (John 2:8–10) for the finer wine to be served late in the celebration?

In reality, this miracle—this "sign"—is less about the couple than it is about the ministry of Jesus. John says plainly, "What Jesus did here in Cana of Galilee was the first of the signs through which he revealed his glory" (John 2:11).

When Mary addresses Jesus about the embarrassing realization that the wine has run out before the celebration has ended, the puzzling conversation between Jesus and Mary seems awkward. It is difficult to tell, even in the original language of the Gospel, whether the address of Jesus to Mary begins with a term of endearment or whether he is resistant to being asked to intervene. But the Gospel writer is certain that this is a beginning—that the "hour" (v. 4) that is initiated at this event finds its fulfillment in the death and resurrection of Jesus.

In John 12:23, in the last day or so before his crucifixion, after the Greeks request to see Jesus, he responds, "The hour has come for the Son of Man to be glorified." We must not miss this: everything that happens throughout the life and ministry of Jesus leads to the cross. The cross is not an intrusion on an otherwise-planned completion of his ministry. It is the whole point. Beginning with that wedding miracle, the way is clear to Jesus, even though it is not clear to his closest followers. There is a mission to be carried out, and the cross is the means by which he will be glorified. In this Lenten journey, we must not overlook the stark reality that the cross is both the mission *and* the model of life with Jesus.

In a season in Christian history when the message of Jesus is so often co-opted by radical, self-serving individualism, the life and ministry of Jesus must become instructive for us. Life in Christ is a life in mission. It is the mission of Jesus. It is a mission of suffering love, of humble, other-serving relationships, of deep surrender of our own self-interest to the interests of others (Philippians 2:4).

Since his hour, our life has purpose. Our purpose is his mission, his way, on his terms. Oh, I think we need to pray!

—JCM

REFLECTION & PRACTICE

01 No one plans a trip to a sign that says, "Disney World: This Way!" The sign *points* us toward our ultimate destination. In the same way, the signs Jesus performs point toward his identity and mission.
- Reflect on the significance and symbolism of Jesus's first sign being performed at a wedding.
- How might the themes of abundance, provision, celebration, and covenant draw our imaginations toward the marriage supper of the Lamb?

02 While the sign ultimately reveals the glory of Jesus, it is performed in the context of service to others. How might our obedience to God both bring glory to God and bless others? Can the two be separated?

03 From the earliest days of his ministry, Jesus demonstrates continual attention and submission to the mission of the Father, performed in self-giving humility and love.
- Do we see our lives through the lens of obedience to and participation in the mission of God?
- Is our obedience marked by self-giving love and humility, or self-righteousness individualism?

PRAYER

Lord, thank you for your faithfulness to the mission of God for our sake and the sake of the world. We also give thanks for your obedience to the method of God: self-giving love and service. We confess that we often drift from your mission as we are consumed by the siren call of other priorities. Even when we seek to participate in your mission, we confess that our motives and methods are not always pure. Convict us of our pride and self-righteousness, that we might love and serve as you did—to the end that others are drawn into your loving embrace.

TUESDAY

AM Psalm: 45

PM Psalms: 47, 48

Deuteronomy 9:4–12

John 2:13–22

Hebrews 3:1–11

A warm and fuzzy Jesus is not an option for us in the Gospel passage for today. This story jars us, unsettling some of the assumptions we easily make about "gentle Jesus, meek and mild." We live in an age when some Christians so magnify the love of Jesus that there is no threat in encountering him. But at some level, we must contend with passages in Scripture that are not comfortable—and perhaps even not safe!

The cherished story of Noah and the ark is often made appealing and nostalgic. But the reality is that God is intent on destroying humanity and beginning over again with Noah and his family (see Genesis 6:5–7). And who can forget the account of God's reaction to the people of Israel creating a golden calf while Moses is on the mountain communing with God, receiving the tablets of the Law? In today's passage from Deuteronomy, Moses tells the Israelites, "At Horeb you aroused the LORD's wrath so that he was angry enough to destroy you" (verse 8).

But in the Gospel passage for today is a critical insight that underlies the entire story of God: God passionately cares about all people—even broken and sinful people. While God hates sin and its power to destroy people and distort creation, God has always longed for relationship with God's highest expression of creation—humankind.

The challenge of Jesus to the money changers in the temple is that this house—the temple—is intended to be a house of prayer for all people (see Mark 11:17). It is likely that the location of the tables Jesus overturns is in the court of the gentiles. Those gentile God fearers have to contend with all the clutter. The money changers, the animals, the tables, baskets, and pens are everywhere. The place where anyone who is not a Jew can come to worship the God of the Jews—the Creator of heaven and earth—is overrun with merchandise.

When we make it difficult or impossible for people to access God, we alienate ourselves from those people and also from God. The nature and character of God are to reach everyone with redemptive grace. When we have callous disregard for people we consider "less than," or "other," or unacceptable, or contemptible, we make it difficult or impossible for them to see God through us. In doing so, we put barriers up between ourselves and God.

Some of our passages for today remind us that it is possible to offend God. That may be one of the most important purposes for the season of Lent. We reflect on our journey. We engage in introspection and self-examination. We ask ourselves the painfully difficult questions: Is my spiritual journey, consciously or unconsciously, hindered by my disregard of the needs of others around me? Am I erecting barriers that hinder others from access to God and God's grace? Is my expectation that, as long as I am sincere, what I do is okay? God's own people, having been given the responsibility to be a light to the gentiles, are putting obstacles in the way of the gentiles entering the space designated as their initial approach to Israel's God.

We do prefer the gentle Jesus to the Jesus who overturns tables and scatters coins and animals. But maybe we need to have an occasional encounter with the Jesus who disturbs our complacency.

—JCM

REFLECTION & PRACTICE

01 In Jesus's angry, destructive behavior in the temple, we are reminded of
the Old Testament wrath of God.
- What parallels exist between Jesus's behavior here and God's
behavior in the Old Testament, particularly in today's Old
Testament passages?
- What common purpose lies at the heart of divine anger?

02 The purchases being made in the temple provide people with what
is needed to make appropriate sacrifices to God. Yet God is not
pleased. Read Hosea 6:6. How do sacrificial traditions like the temple
marketplace work against the intent of the sacrifices themselves?

03 God reserves God's deepest anger for the people of God and the
pattern of welcoming the blessings of God while neglecting the God-
given vocation of justice, witness, and radical inclusion.
- How do we slip into this same pattern? Do we, consciously or
unconsciously, prevent others from encountering God by our
myopic focus on our individual spiritual journeys?
- What might it mean to "kick out the money changers" in our
corporate faith practice today? Who might find welcome in that
cleared space?

PRAYER

*Lord, we confess that we are quick to embrace your blessings and slow to
practice our vocation as people of light and justice in your beloved world. In
humility, we acknowledge that, like Israel, we are often blind to how our sin
often misshapes faith practices and hurts people who are precious to you.
Forgive our selfish spirituality and reorient our hearts toward justice, mercy,
and inclusion for the sake of the world you love.*

WEDNESDAY

AM Psalm: 119:49–72

PM Psalms: 49, 53

Deuteronomy 9:13–21

John 2:23–3:15

Hebrews 3:12–19

One of the greatest dangers we face is when we begin to worship the gifts of God rather than worshiping the God who gives. In Deuteronomy 9, Moses reminds the people of Israel about their bowing to the golden calf. The account of the event itself can be found in Exodus 32. It details the people bringing gold earrings to Aaron, who fashions the molten gold into the image of a calf—and then they worship the calf! That is when things fall apart for Israel.

Remember where the gold earrings came from? When the people are ready to escape from Egypt, God tells them to ask the Egyptians for gold and silver. God makes the Egyptians "favorably disposed" toward the people, and they are given what they ask for. As the account states it, "they plundered the Egyptians" (Exodus 12:36). The gold and silver are a gift from God! So, what do they do with the gifts God provided? They begin to worship the golden calf that has been made from those very gifts.

It is always a temptation to treasure what we can see or touch. When Nicodemus comes to Jesus, he is impressed with the signs Jesus has been performing. He acknowledges that God was with Jesus. The challenge Jesus issues to Nicodemus is that Nicodemus only sees the surface.

Unless he is born of the Spirit, he will not see what is really going on. The kingdom of God has come, and the very people who should recognize it and know it best—the Jewish religious leaders—are blind to what is happening. When the people in Jerusalem see the signs he is performing, they believe in his name, but Jesus knows that deep within they are not yet able to see the meaning behind the signs.

One of the liabilities of familiarity is the capacity to be committed to our patterns of worship, our structures and traditions, and to miss the point of it all. Until, and unless, we have an encounter with the Spirit of God in a deeply reorienting receptivity to the Spirit, we will operate on the level of what we can see or touch. God desires to so encounter us that we begin to know God! "Flesh gives birth to flesh," said Jesus to Nicodemus in John 3:6, "but the Spirit gives birth to spirit."

The Lenten journey has no objective more essential than this—that we may know God. The practices of Lent (self-examination, self-denial, service to others, etc.) are not ends in themselves. They are the means by which we are invited and encouraged to receive the Spirit, to walk with the Spirit, and to be led by the Spirit.

O God, give us eyes to see your kingdom!

—JCM

REFLECTION & PRACTICE

01 Pause and reflect: What gifts has God given to you? How does your life reflect gratitude for these gifts?

02 The people of Israel abuse their gold—the physical expressions of God's gift of deliverance—when they are afraid and uncertain.
- How do difficult circumstances make us vulnerable to abusing the gifts of God?
- How might we guard against idolatry of those gifts, even in the midst of confusion, uncertainty, and fear?

03 Jesus invites Nicodemus to move beyond what he can see and touch by being born of the Spirit. Only by encountering the transforming Spirit of God can Nicodemus begin to understand what God is doing in Christ.
- What practices might help us cultivate a spirit receptive to the gift that is the Holy Spirit?
- How might the Holy Spirit want to reorient us with new vision this Lenten season?

PRAYER

Lord, we confess that, while we welcome your gifts, we do not always steward them faithfully. Our fear, confusion, and lack of understanding lead us to idolatry. We desire to know and follow you, yet we are unsettled by complete surrender. Control feels more comfortable. Send your Spirit to empower us to trust. Reorient us toward your coming kingdom, and give us eyes to see you and your beloved world rightly.

THURSDAY

AM Psalms: 50, 59, 60

PM Psalms: 19, 46

Deuteronomy 9:23–10:5

John 3:16–21

Hebrews 4:1–10

John 3:16 is one of the most loved and recognized verses in all of Scripture. Young children are taught to recite it. It shows up on billboards, at sports venues, on banners, and on clothing. Many commentators state that this verse is the concise summation of the Gospel of John. But how we read the verse is crucial. It can bring great hope when understood as the description of the universal reach of the gospel of Jesus Christ and of the stunning magnitude of God's love for all humanity. But the larger passage in the Gospel reading for today places before us a stark reality: our decision to believe and our willingness to place our trust in God's love as it is revealed in the gift of God's Son create an immediate, grace-enabled entry into life in breadth, depth, length, and height. It is eternal life in the best sense. But it is also true, at a profound level, that to choose not to believe is to enter into darkness, into condemnation, into judgment. It is not delayed judgment. It is immediate. A deathliness has already begun that will find confirmation in that final judgment about which Jesus speaks in John 5:28–29.

The risk of wrestling with these words in John 3 is that we can find ourselves overwhelmed with dread and with the fear of judgment. Knowing our own frailty and sinfulness, we fixate on the dire consequences of what happens if we don't believe. We can descend into a depressive fear of living, consumed by a continuing sense of condemnation. But that was not the purpose for these gracious words from Jesus. His whole point was the magnitude of God's love—the breadth and depth of that love, demonstrated in the gift of Jesus for the redemption of the world.

The season of Lent is intended for us to participate in a heart-deep preparation to celebrate the resurrection of Jesus with anticipation and joy on Easter Sunday. We are gazing into the astounding love of God and responding to God's invitation to embrace that love. We are examining our hearts and shaping our lives to align even more deeply with the depths of that love. The self-examination and self-denial of this season are never intended to deepen our fear. Rather, they are intended to awaken our joy. They open our minds and hearts to a greater grasp of all that God's Spirit desires to provide to us as we seek a deeper walk with the Risen One.

Oh, yes. Dig deep. Examine your life, your spirit, your attitudes, and your practices. But never forget the love. Never overlook the motive behind the cross. This is love as never seen before, and it is available to all. Take it! Take all you need! It is for you. And it is free!

—JCM

REFLECTION & PRACTICE

01 Jesus speaks not only of life that is to come but also of life that begins now. As we live into the truth God's action in Christ, we come into the light in this time and place.

- How does this idea differ from the idea that eternal life only describes life beyond death?
- Where have you seen the life of the age to come breaking into your life now? Your family? Your community?

02 If eternal life can begin now, so too can the consequences of rejecting God's love in Christ. How does persistently resisting God's invitation malform us from the inside out, both now and long term?

03 The disciplines of self-denial and Spirit-guided self-examination are intended to bring us into a deeper understanding of God and God's love for us, as well as attune our ears to the Spirit's call to continued surrender.

- What is the voice of Love revealing to you through the disciplines of Lent?
- How are you being challenged to trust more deeply and obey more completely?

PRAYER

Lord, thank you for your immeasurable love for us. You came to us before we even knew our need. You come to us still, wooing us back to yourself. Soften our hearts. Unstop our ears. Nurture in us a deep, abiding trust. As we learn to trust your love, banish the fear of judgment that entangles us. You are worthy of our trust and obedience. We give you permission to heal and restore us, convict and correct us.

FRIDAY

AM Psalms: 40, 54

PM Psalm: 51

Deuteronomy 10:12–22

John 3:22–36

Hebrews 4:11–16

John Sugg and I were college roommates, sang in the college quartet together, and spent many long hours traveling across the southeast U.S. with the quartet, visiting churches and recruiting students. We were also privileged to serve as best men in each other's weddings. Our friendship has endured, and to this day, more than fifty years after our first meeting, we still communicate with each other frequently.

As my best man, John took special care to watch out for my wife, Susan, and me. Our mutual friends, some of whom were my groomsmen, were intent on making a memorable impact on our honeymoon. John, who was also friends with the groomsmen, was aware of their plans. In the final moments before Susan and I drove away from the reception, John slipped up to me, giving me a quiet caution about a hidden "gift" in our car. "As soon as you can," he said, "stop and remove this 'gift' from under your front seat." And we did. As a friend of the bridegroom, John was more intent on looking after Susan and me than he was in protecting the plans of our other friends.

John the Baptist has followers who are jealous to protect John's stature and reputation. When the crowds begin to follow Jesus, John's disciples want to warn John about the competition. But John's loyalty is to the "bridegroom"—the one to whom his ministry has been pointing from the very beginning. "He (Jesus) is the reason I came here in the first place," John is saying.

It is time for John's disciples to make a shift in their loyalty. Their hope lies in what Jesus has come to accomplish, not in what John has been called to do. John was to prepare the way. Jesus is the Way to whom John has been pointing. Their hope is not in their loyalty to John but in their recognition that God is making God's self fully known in and through Jesus.

In our Lenten journey, it may be necessary for us to face the need for a shift in our loyalties. If we are driven by self-interest, our following Christ may be for the sake of what we get out of it—yet Christ desires for us to be so radically committed to him that our first priorities are to know him and to make him known. The Gospel text for today implies a need to be focused, determined, and unwavering. This phrase of unknown origin expresses it well: "My goal is God. Not joy, nor peace, not even blessing, but my God."

—JCM

REFLECTION & PRACTICE

01 The disciples of John the Baptist are protective of their leader. They have forgotten that John's ministry is not an end to itself but a preparation for something greater.
- In what ways does the church occasionally lose sight of the ultimate end—namely, elevating Christ?
- How do our loyalties drift from Christ alone? What might it look like to re-center our loyalties on Jesus?

02 John is not flattered by his disciples' protectiveness. Rather, with complete clarity, he says, "He must become greater; I must become less."
- How does this response go against the grain of culture?
- In what ways should John's statement be true in our lives? How can we elevate Jesus over and above ourselves or our ministries?

03 John calls his disciples to ground their hope not in him but in the One who is coming after him.
- In what or whom do we root our hope? In the church as we have known and experienced it? In specific political outcomes?
- What attitudes or behaviors might reveal misplaced hope?

PRAYER

Lord, how easily we lose sight of our purpose to glorify and elevate you. Consumed by our work—even the good work we do for the church—our loyalties slide from you, our crucified Savior, to our own agendas. Forgive us when we root our hope in anything but you alone. May we become less that you might become greater, in our lives and in the world.

SATURDAY

AM Psalm: 55

PM Psalms: 138, 139

Deuteronomy 11:18–28

John 4:1–26

Hebrews 5:1–10

The story of Jesus and the Samaritan woman in the Gospel of John is a familiar one. We love it as an example of Jesus reaching outside the "in crowd," into the brokenness of a woman from a despised race and a competing religious tradition. Though having common roots with the Jews, the Samaritans were a part of what is known as the lost tribes of Israel. They were the remnants of what had been the people of Israel who separated from Judah centuries before. In 2 Kings 17:24–41 is a description of how the Samaritans came into being. In the final verse is the poignant phrase, "Even while these people were worshiping the LORD, they were serving their idols."

The passage from Deuteronomy for today states with stunning clarity the risk of adulterated worship. Moses sets before the people of God a blessing and a curse. There is a blessing for worshiping and obeying the words of God—Yahweh, the God of Israel. But there is a curse if they disobey the commands of the Lord and follow other gods.

When Jesus encounters the woman, she discloses a hopeful eschatology. A Messiah is coming, she says. He will explain everything and—perhaps, in her mind—straighten out the matter of where and how

God is to be worshiped. Jesus's response makes clear that worship requires more than the "right place." Worship requires an undivided heart. "God is spirit," Jesus says, "and his worshipers must worship in the Spirit and in truth" (John 4:24).

The risk of adulterated worship is greater than we know and could be far more likely than we wish. The passage from 2 Kings 17 makes clear that the problem is not that the Samaritans have rejected the worship of the Lord; it is that they are not exclusive in their worship. Even while they worship the Lord, "they were serving their idols" (v. 41).

Today, we can become distracted from worship by many other things, even legitimate things. When our work becomes our idol, we can't worship God in truth. When our family—as legitimate and necessary as family is to the kingdom of God—becomes an idol, demanding an allegiance that hinders our worship of the Lord, even a good thing can become an idol. When possessions or position or pleasure or nation or any other legitimate thing hinders our ability to worship without entanglement, we may be dealing with an idol.

Lent is intended to help us focus our attention on the journey of our Lord toward the cross. It is a means by which we may search our hearts to the depths in order to examine our lives, motives, worship, and practices. We seek to identify with Christ and to join him on the journey of unwavering obedience to the will of God for us and through us for others. Read again John 4:23–24. Let's become the kind of worshipers the Father seeks.

—JCM

REFLECTION & PRACTICE

01 The Samaritan people find themselves separated from God not because of failure to worship God but because of a failure to worship *only* God.
- How does a refusal to worship God exclusively ultimately distance us from God?
- The Samaritans' disobedience results in generations of spiritual confusion. How might our rebellion, whether active or passive, bear toxic fruit in generations to come?

02 Jesus has no interest in debating the right place to worship. He is far more concerned about the state of the worshiper's heart. What nonessentials do we wrongly elevate to essential? How are we tempted to fixate on the right facility, the right ministry style, or other things that miss the point of worship?

03 The most dangerous idols are not the obvious, evil patterns and devotions. The far more dangerous idols are the good things in our lives that we elevate beyond their appropriate place.
- What good things easily become idols in our lives?
- How can we guard against the idolatry of the good to protect our hearts for the best—worship of God alone? What role might our community of faith play in our discernment?

PRAYER

Lord, we confess that our hearts are often divided. We desire to worship you in Spirit and in truth, but we acknowledge our tendency to elevate even good things beyond their proper place. You alone are worthy of our hearts' true worship. Make known to us the idols of our hearts, that we might confess and rectify our lives by the power of your Spirit.

SECOND SUNDAY

IN LENT

AM Psalms: 24, 29

PM Psalms: 8, 84

Jeremiah 1:1–10

Mark 3:31–4:9

1 Corinthians 3:11–23

Don't forget to worship. Yes, this is the Lenten season, and it is characterized by self-examination, self-denial, and service to others. But on Sundays, the focus is on worship. Fasting and self-denial are laid aside for this day in honor of the majestic God who is the King of glory.

The collection of passages for this day are soul-lifting. God is present, and God's power is on full display. Psalm 29:4 declares, "The voice of the LORD is powerful; the voice of the LORD is majestic." Later on, "The LORD is enthroned as King forever" (v. 10). And even yet, says the psalmist, the Lord considers us, cares for us, and has put everything under our feet (8:4, 6). God knows us intimately, yet treasures us deeply.

In the Mark passage for today is the parable of the sower. It is a familiar story that is often the source of searching, challenging sermons. There is great risk in sowing precious seed. The sower finds that some of the seeds are wasted. A lot of sermonic emphasis is focused on this passage as a challenge to the hearers: what kind of soil are we?

But across all the passages for today are powerful reminders that the God we worship is not contained in finite spaces or limited in resources or unaware of our existence (Jeremiah 1:5). God made it all, and God is in it all. God is also at work in it all, even when we don't see it.

Paul, writing to a conflicted church, reminds them that their loyalties to one leader or another are of little significance. What matters most is that the message of redemption and transformation is abundantly sufficient. "All things are yours," he writes. In other words, everything they brought to you through the power of the Holy Spirit, by the grace of God, is yours, "and you are of Christ, and Christ is of God" (1 Corinthians 3:21, 23).

Many Christians live in a state of fear and uncertainty. Some are overwhelmed by the evil around them, thanks to the news bearing constant stories of devastation, disease, war, and crime. It becomes easy to focus on the bad news, the "rocky soil," or the thorns threatening to choke out any hope that God's grace is at work in our world. But Jesus made it clear. The Sower is at work, and the seed is being scattered. In the final analysis, the shallow soil and the threatening thorns will prove to have had no lasting impact on the Sower's intent. The crop will grow and produce far more than we knew or expected!

"And in his temple all cry, 'Glory!'" (Psalm 29:9c).

—JCM

REFLECTION & PRACTICE

01 Psalm 29 leans heavily on imagery from creation, describing the lordship of God through mastery over all created things.
- How have you experienced God in creation?
- How might you intentionally make space to be present to God's good creation today? (Some suggestions: go for a walk, take in a sunset, or snuggle with a pet.)

02 In the parable of the sower, the farmer is extravagant in his sowing. With seemingly reckless abandon, he sows generously in the hope that the seeds will take root.
- How have you experienced God's lavish outpouring of grace, mercy, and love in your life?
- How might we till the soil of our hearts to make it more nourishing for what God wants to plant in our lives?

03 In today's epistle, Paul describes us as "God's temple." We often interpret this language as applying to us as individuals—but the Greek is plural. We together, as a family of faith, constitute God's temple, the dwelling place of God.
- How might this vision of the church as the dwelling place of God deepen our understanding of corporate worship and community?
- How can you commit yourself more fully to the body of Christ?

PRAYER

Lord, we worship you today. You are Creator, Master of the universe. We are sustained by your generous provision and care. You have formed us and continue to form us, into your dwelling place. May we respond in faithful obedience to your call on our lives, this day and every day.

MONDAY

AM Psalms: 56, 57, 58

PM Psalms: 64, 65

Jeremiah 1:11–19

John 4:27–42

Romans 1:1–15

Imagine the shock. To see their leader sitting alone with a woman—and a despised Samaritan woman at that. The disciples do not speak, but the expression on their faces, the suspicion in their eyes, and the disdain hovering about their lips ignite shame and anger in the woman's heart. But then she looks to Jesus again. The sting of their judgment is washed away by a crashing wave of love. She rushes back to the village to share her joy at being seen and loved by the One.

Afraid to ask questions, the disciples turn instead to the practical: "Rabbi, eat something" (John 4:31). They do not understand that Jesus has just feasted—not on bread or figs but on the nourishing, sustaining food that is doing the will of God. Jesus sees what they cannot, blinded as they are by racism and prejudice: the harvest is ripe. God is on the move, even among those they would deem unworthy—perhaps especially among these.

Just as the disciples would have recognized the signs of an impending harvest, we recognize signs as well: Leaves transforming from pliant and green to crisp and orange indicate the change of seasons. Black clouds billowing across a blue August sky warn us of a thunderstorm. Yet, like the disciples, do we miss the signs of God at work among us? Are we so beholden to our vision of God and God's way of acting in the world that we fail to grasp the transformation unfolding in our midst?

Samaritans stream to the well, eager to discover the identity of this man, Jesus. While they are initially captivated by the woman's witness, ultimately they come to know and trust Jesus as Messiah for themselves. They proclaim what no Jew, save John the Baptist, has yet uttered: "This man really is the Savior of the world" (v. 42)! The disciples in closest proximity to Jesus have yet to grasp this truth. The outsiders— the "unworthy," those with nothing to commend themselves to Jesus— recognize him first.

The gospel narrative will continue. More wondrous signs will be performed, far more dramatic than a prophetic insight into a woman's broken story. Yet, even when confronted by miraculous signs, no crowd of insiders will respond to Jesus with the level of devotion and trust as that village of Samaritans who so quickly declare him Lord and Christ.

Perhaps the Samaritans' experience of mistreatment and rejection gave them a deep hunger for God's saving action in whatever form it might come. Perhaps the disdain and abuse they endured for generations for their "impure" heritage has cracked their hearts open, making them ready to receive Love in their midst. The excluded cannot afford to be bound by expectations and decorum. The disinherited have no agenda to drive forward except their desire for wholeness and acceptance.

As we journey with Christ toward the cross once again this Lenten season, perhaps our vision of God's work on earth as it is in heaven might be expanded if we pause a moment to sit at the well, to gather with those different from us, those excluded by the system, those even considered "unworthy," and listen. Perhaps we will begin to recognize the riches of a ripe harvest among us. Through these sisters and brothers, may we know hunger, that we might be satisfied by the feast that is doing the will of God.

—SDL

REFLECTION & PRACTICE

01 In the northern hemisphere, the Lenten season begins in winter and takes us toward or into early spring. The earth is beginning to brighten with new life. Change is occurring.

- What signs of seasonal change are you beginning to see? It may be the earth itself, or those caring for the earth and preparing for spring.
- Can you allow yourself to see something in the normal change of seasons that might surprise you with new appreciation for what is happening?
- As you look around, what changes do you see that reflect the refreshing presence of the kingdom of God at work?

02 In our spiritual journey we are often so accustomed to what we see and know that we may miss something new that God is doing.

- How might you open yourself to see something that God is doing that is a surprise to you?
- Describe a time when God was revealed through someone you didn't expect.

03 It is easy to miss the work of God among people who do not fit our preconceptions of what it means to be worthy or capable.

- Where is God working in ways that are uncomfortable for you?
- What is God saying to you about those who are shunned by others as unacceptable or repulsive?
- How can you reflect God's love among those people?

PRAYER

Father, we are so easily conditioned to see you at work in the ways we have always experienced you and among the people we are comfortable being around. Will you open our eyes to the harvest around us—the people in whom and through whom you are revealing yourself to the world? May our prejudices be faced, our preconceptions challenged, and our love expanded to reach as widely as your love expanded to reach us.

TUESDAY

AM Psalms: 61, 62

PM Psalm: 68

Jeremiah 2:1–13

John 4:43–54

Romans 1:16–25

In today's Gospel reading, Jesus returns to Galilee to fanfare. Not only has news of the sign in Cana surely spread, but the people have also heard of his shocking behavior in the temple, driving out the money changers and vendors who transformed the court of gentiles into a marketplace.

Soon after his return to Cana, Jesus is met by a frantic father who is desperate for healing for his gravely ill son. Nothing, not even his status as a royal official, has been able to procure the healing his son needs.

Jesus's initial response to the father seems callous: "Unless you see signs and wonders, you will not believe." Does he not care about the suffering of this child or his parent? But Jesus's response is not merely to the worried father but also to all the people clamoring for his attention. Jesus is growing impatient with "signs faith"—that is, devotion contingent upon what he can do for the people and their boundless needs, but with no depth.

It is not a new phenomenon: humankind seeking after God for what God can provide for them but withholding unconditional worship and devotion. In Jeremiah 2, God reminds Israel of their former devotion, how they followed God through the wilderness. The intimacy was sweet, Israel's love like that of a bride. But, once settled in the promised land, when Israel no longer depended on God for their daily bread, their hearts wandered. The prophet describes Israel as forsaking the Lord, "the spring of living water," and digging "their own cisterns . . . that cannot hold water," an expression for idolatrous self-sufficiency (Jeremiah 2:13). In Romans 1, Paul cites the same pattern yet again. In spite of God's revelation through creation, humankind has turned from worship of the Creator to worship of what they have created themselves.

In all three texts, the sin present in human hearts makes itself known. We seek deliverance but refuse to surrender lordship. We scramble after what we need to survive but withhold our devotion, obedience, and trust. Instead of resting securely at the spring of Living Water, we dig our own cisterns, ignoring their cracks, convinced we are better off fending for ourselves.

But that father in John 4, knees in the dust at Jesus's feet, has no interest in building his own cistern. The illusion of self-sufficiency has passed, dismantled by the harrowing illness of his child. "Sir, come down before my child dies" (v. 49).

In spite of Jesus's exasperation with "signs faith," he acts as God always acts—mercifully. "Go, your son will live" (v. 50). Sheer grace.

And the father's response? "The man took Jesus at his word and departed" (v. 50).

This Lenten season, may we move beyond "signs faith," in which we offer God our conditional obedience, and give ourselves over fully to this trustworthy King. May we rest at the spring of Living Water instead of frantically digging our own, and take Jesus at his word.

—SDL

REFLECTION & PRACTICE

The desperation of a parent with a gravely sick child paints a vivid picture of anxiety, fear, and vulnerability. The request of the father is for healing. The response of Jesus is revelation.

- Rev. Lobdell describes the healing of the royal official's son as "sheer grace." What does that mean to your understanding of this event?
- What distinction do you see between the healing and the Healer? Where should our focus be in this story?

In today's texts, people reveal conditional, signs-based faith as well as idolatrous self-sufficiency.

- In what ways are we guilty of conditional faith, putting down shallow roots when we get what we desire, only to rip them up when we are disappointed?
- Unlike the people in Jeremiah, the father abandons self-sufficiency, knowing he is powerless in the face of his son's illness. What might it look like for us to surrender self-sufficiency and entrust ourselves fully to God?

It is not unusual for us to ask God to work—to perform "signs and wonders."

- What is the significance of the phrase in verse 50: "The man took Jesus at his word and departed"?
- What is the focus of the man and his household when they "believe"?

PRAYER

We are so easily enamored of answers to our prayers that come with thunder or lightning, Father. Help us in this journey to reorient our minds and hearts not so much on what you can do as on who you are. Teach us in this season, as we open our hearts and minds to you, to see you. May our hearts become warmed by your character and your presence more than by the satisfaction of our demands that you do things in the way we ask or expect.

49

WEDNESDAY

AM Psalm: 72

PM Psalm: 119:73–96

Jeremiah 3:6–8

John 5:1–18

Romans 1:28–2:11

Every Jewish festival with its unique practices and proclamations, every recitation of God's deliverance and mercy invited the Jewish people to remember the lordship of God and to entrust their lives into God's hands once again even in the midst of oppression from empires like Rome.

As a faithful Jewish man, Jesus participates in the festivals alongside his fellow Israelites. In John 5, Jesus leaves the typical festival throng of worshipers to intentionally seek out and walk among what Matthew 25:40 would call "the least of these."

Having seen Jesus's mercy in action through the first four chapters of the Gospel of John, we readers are not surprised by the healing of the man who has been so long burdened by his state of paralysis. The small insertion at the end of verse 9, letting us know it was the Sabbath, seems like a minor comment serving the sole purpose of providing color to the story. But the impending controversy, rooted in Sabbath regulations, reveals that comment to be central to the narrative. The subsequent vitriolic reaction of the Jewish leadership feels foreign and entirely unjust.

For the Jewish people, Sabbath observance was a primary identity marker. No other culture practiced a day of rest. How could they afford to in the ancient world, where survival hinged on dogged, endless work? The Sabbath served as a bold theological declaration: *God is the source. We are not. God provides. We participate and receive.*

But, as often happens in a world marked by sin and death, what was given as a gift was malformed into a measuring stick, even a disciplinary rod. Sabbath practice became an indicator of who was in and who was out, who was righteous and who was outside the bounds of God's family.

Before we shake our heads in disgust at the Jewish leaders' behavior, it would be wise to sit under today's epistle reading. Paul describes the sin of others in vivid detail, working insiders into a frenzy of judgment and self-righteousness. Then, out of nowhere, comes 2:1: "You, therefore, have no excuse, you who pass judgment on someone else, for at whatever point you judge another, you are condemning yourself, because you who pass judgment do the same things."

We who are tempted to scoff at the Jewish leaders' desire to control and narrowly define God's work in the world: are our hearts closed to the stirring of the Spirit? We grimace at the bitter heart of the man healed who persists in hardheartedness and sin even after he is delivered from his affliction. But do we also choose rancor over gratitude? Resentment over celebration?

This Lenten season, may we suspend our judgments and instead lift our hearts up to the Lord for holy examination and healing.

—*SDL*

REFLECTION & PRACTICE

01 The fact that Jesus healed on the Sabbath is not a minor point in this Gospel story. Rev. Lobdell says, "What was given as a gift was malformed into a measuring stick, even a disciplinary rod."

- Where have you seen a gift of God turned into a measuring stick or a disciplinary rod?
- How do you respond to this statement: The Sabbath served as a bold theological declaration: *God is the source. We are not. God provides. We participate and receive.*

02 The apostle Paul in Romans strongly cautions us to beware the tendency to become judge and jury in regard to the behavior of others.

- What steps might we take to avoid a critical spirit regarding the practices of others?
- Where is the balance between loving concern and condemnation? What practices might guide us in discerning that difference?

PRAYER

It is so easy, Father, to have such zeal for your holiness, and ours, that we become bitter and angry toward those we judge as disregarding your Word and bringing reproach on your church. Help us have a discerning spirit while guarding against becoming judgmental. May our love for you be demonstrated in our love toward others. May we allow you the responsibility to exercise grace and mercy when we would prefer to administer judgment.

THURSDAY

AM Psalms: 70, 71

PM Psalm: 74

Jeremiah 4:9–10, 19–28

John 5:19–29

Romans 2:12–24

Contrary to the modern argument, we are not solitary beings. We are inextricably bound up in our relationships with others. We could flee to the farthest corners of the earth and still remain a daughter, a son, a cousin, a father. I will never cease to be the daughter of Brad and Debbie. My life has been shaped irrevocably by my relation to them. I know Jesus because they introduced me to him. I see the world in certain ways because of their influence. Our connections to one another, whether chosen or biological, shape us.

In John 5, the religious leaders are enraged because Jesus dared to call God his Father, "making himself equal with God" (v. 18). Instead of redirecting his language, Jesus presses further into it. He is the Son, beloved of the Father, who acts in accordance with the will of the Father. They are united in love, which is expressed in a common mission. As deep and complete as their divine intimacy is, it is not a closed circuit. We are invited into the family as we "hear the word" of Jesus and "believe him who sent" Jesus. The invitation into this sacred space of love is transformative; we "cross over from death to life" (v. 24).

There is no need to parse out from Jesus's language when he is speaking of the future, bodily resurrection or the present, spiritual resurrection. The point is clear: God is unleashing God's life-restoring power through the Son, beginning now and stretching into eternity. Lives marked by death and death's fruit—anger, hate, judgment, hypocrisy, greed, hunger for power—are now marked by signs of life: forgiveness, inclusion, mercy, and faithfulness. As we trust more deeply and allow ourselves to be loved and fully known, we are transformed into the image of Christ in ever-increasing degrees.

There is no mention of Sabbath adherence—the inflammatory issue that initiated this confrontation between Jesus and the religious leaders—not because Sabbath doesn't matter but because it is not at the heart of faithfulness. Faithful Sabbath practice is an expression of abiding trust in the King of the universe, not a means by which to exclude others. Jesus will not allow the leaders to weaponize the gift of the Sabbath. He is not interested in keeping an eternal scorecard. Rather, Jesus desires far more: followers whose lives are marked by the divine love of the Trinity, who bear the family resemblance to the world.

We no longer measure the steps a person takes on Sunday to determine if they have exceeded the bounds of rest. We no longer publicly chide someone for laboring by carrying a mat. Lest we think ourselves beyond the religious leaders and their ability to miss the point entirely, however, let us consider the words of today's epistle text. Do we—who are convinced we are guides to the blind and light to those in darkness—embody the divine love of the Trinity? Or is the name of God blasphemed among the world because of us?

—*SDL*

REFLECTION & PRACTICE

01 "Contrary to the modern argument, we are not solitary beings. We are
inextricably bound up in our relationships with others."

- How does this statement resonate with your own journey? What
shaping influences have been at work in your life?
- How do the words of Jesus in describing his relationship with
the Father inform your understanding of our relationship with
the Father?

02 Jesus desires followers whose lives are marked by "the divine love of
the Trinity, who bear the family resemblance to the world."

- How does Paul's caution to the Jewish Christians in Romans
12:21–23 inform how we might live?
- How may we honor God's name in our interaction with other
people?

PRAYER

*Father, we seek to be genuine expressions of your love in our broken
world. We confess that we often find ourselves judging, critiquing, or
condemning others who live in ways that offend us. Teach us how we may
live authentically before you, reflecting your holiness in our words and deeds,
while we also bear your love toward all people.*

FRIDAY

AM Psalm: 69

PM Psalm: 73

Jeremiah 5:1–9

John 5:30–47

Romans 2:25–3:18

During my time serving the church abroad, I visited a small Italian town with friends for a day at the beach. On our way to the water, we saw a small sign that pointed toward a set of stairs. The sign read: "Temple of Diana." We were intrigued and decided to follow the sign, assured that the temple was at the top of the stairs and that our side journey would take ten minutes at the most. An hour later we arrived at the ruins, sweaty and breathless, having climbed the highest hill in the area. The journey was not what we anticipated, but the ruins were remarkable and the view unmatched.

Imagine if, upon seeing the sign, we had rejoiced and set up camp—right there in front of the sign. Imagine if we had taken group photos around the sign and posted them online, telling all our friends about the wonders of the Temple of Diana. How foolish that would've been! No one mistakes the *sign* for the *destination,* right?

In today's Gospel reading, Jesus calls out his listeners for doing that very thing: mistaking the signs for the destination. Moses, the great leader and instrument of God's gift of the law, was a sign who pointed to the coming Christ. He was not the destination, the arriving point of God's revelation. The law that they cherish so deeply was also a sign that revealed

Jesus as King—if only their hearts were softened to perceive it. Their devotion to the Torah (the Scripture) had become idolatrous in that they forgot its purpose: to guide them to God's revelation—a revelation that climaxes in the unveiling of Jesus the Christ. The signs cannot give life.

No one consciously decides to glorify the signs and ignore the destination to which the signs point. But, when our hearts become captive to glory that does not come from God, and when we prefer the smooth words of false prophets who proclaim empty promises, the love of God is not in our hearts. We become de-centered and, thus, disconnected from the work of God around us, seeking life where it cannot be found.

We too often seek life where it cannot be found, camping out under the signs of the kingdom and failing to journey toward the kingdom itself in faithfulness. Our right living cannot produce life. Even devotion to Scripture cannot bring life. Apart from the enlivening Spirit, the gift of God's revelation in Scripture remains merely a book, easily manipulated to confirm our own agendas and biases. Lest we think ourselves too educated or too wise to fall prey to such illusions, the prophet Jeremiah calls us to account. He roams the streets of Jerusalem, seeking righteous people who fear the Lord. He does not find them among the poor on the streets, nor does he find them among the rich and educated. But even those who "know the way of the Lord" have "broken off the yoke" (Jeremiah 5:5).

What must we do to be saved? Come to Jesus, the Sent One. Abandon empty glory and seek the only glory that matters—the glory that comes from God, revealed through submission and radical, obedient trust.

—*SDL*

REFLECTION & PRACTICE

01 While we may treasure the law of God, Jesus makes it clear that the law
   was a signpost, not the destination (John 5:46).
   - In what ways could we miss the point as we seek to live by
     God's law?
   - What is the purpose of the law of God? How can we best embrace
     the wonder of those powerful words?

02 The law is a signpost pointing to Christ.
   - How does the law of God point us to Christ? How did Christ
     fulfill what the Law was intended to accomplish?
   - How do we make appropriate use of the law today? Is posting the
     Ten Commandments on monuments the best representation of
     what God intended for the law?

PRAYER

*Father, so often we miss the beauty of your law. We fail to see it as a
perfect expression of your mind, of your love, and of your purposes for us.
Forgive us for seeking to depend on the law for our righteousness. Help
us live in harmony with your law as we are transformed by your Son and
empowered by your Spirit. Teach us how to live like Jesus, who is love,
grace, mercy, and redemption.*

SATURDAY

AM Psalms: 75, 76

PM Psalms: 23, 27

Jeremiah 5:20–31

John 7:1–13

Romans 3:19–31

Expectations. Everybody has them. Our life experiences,
our desires, and our environments incite us to expect certain things
from various people and circumstances. I am usually positive and
hopeful, expecting the best from others and myself. By being hopeful, I
automatically risk disappointment and disillusionment when people let
me down or when I am confronted by the uncomfortable reality that my
interpretation of what is best proves to be wrong.

In today's Gospel, Jesus is intentionally avoiding the crowds with
their idolatrous and ignorant expectations. After he performed the sign of
the loaves and fish, the people sought to crown him king. Jesus does not
demurely refuse their desire; instead, he pushes back aggressively against it
and issues hard teachings, declaring his flesh to be the true bread and his
blood the true drink. Unsettled, the crowds fall away while the leaders lean
into their violent intentions all the more.

In John 7, Jesus's brothers urge him to join them at the Festival
of Booths (or Tabernacles). It is likely that their family has endured
a measure of shame from Jesus's strange, often disturbing teachings.
Whether the brothers want Jesus to vindicate himself and claim his

place as the Christ, or whether they are mocking him in their disbelief is unclear. What is clear is Jesus's response. He will not be who they demand him to be. He will not say what they want to hear. He will not submit to their timeline. His heart is set, his eyes fixed on the calling of his Father to give himself entirely for the sake of the world, to be lifted up—not to a throne but on a cross, for us and for our salvation.

In today's Old Testament text, God speaks to the rebellious people of Israel who "have eyes but do not see, who have ears but do not hear" (Jeremiah 5:21). They have forgotten their identity as a *delivered people*— the recipients of God's saving action. The Lord reserves a particularly sharp rebuke for the prophets and priests, announcing that the prophets lie and "the priests rule by their own authority" (v. 31). Worse yet? "My people love it this way" (v. 31).

Once again this Lenten season, we must allow these difficult texts to read us. How easily we are led astray by our own culturally conditioned expectation! How effortlessly we slide into the comfortable pattern of heeding only the words of our self-imposed echo chambers. We choose self-help over death to self. We elevate voices that say what we want to hear and silence those who dare to point out our hypocrisy. Our expectations reflect devotion to comfort and ease over devotion to a suffering, servant King. Like Israel, we love it that way.

Jeremiah 5 concludes with a simple question: "But what will you do in the end?" What shall we do, indeed? Control or confess? Seek our own way or submit to Jesus?

—*SDL*

REFLECTION & PRACTICE

01 The Gospel passage for today is often confusing for readers. Jesus seems reluctant to go to the Festival of Tabernacles (or Booths), but then he decides to go.
- What might have been behind the response of Jesus to his brothers? Would the expectations of other people be a legitimate cause of concern for Jesus? Why or why not?
- How have our expectations of how God *should* work impacted our prayer lives or our faith journeys?

02 Jesus makes the statement that his time has not yet fully come. What does that statement imply about how Jesus understands his mission? How does the mission of Jesus continue on through us, Jesus's people?

03 Rev. Lobdell warns of the danger of sliding into our self-imposed echo chambers.
- What divergent voices have we silenced because they make us uncomfortable? How might God challenge, convict, or correct us if we step beyond our echo chambers?
- What might hinder our ability to allow God to work for a larger good than our individual needs or wants?

PRAYER

Father, we so easily allow our expectations to blind us to the creative and redemptive work of your Spirit in our lives. Teach us how to move beyond our expectations and demands into a deep and full surrender to your work in and through us. May we move beyond merely asking you to come into our hearts. Instead, may we surrender ourselves into your life, your grace, your mercy, and your work in our world. Lord, work not only in us, but work also through us!

THIRD SUNDAY

IN LENT

AM Psalms: 93, 96

PM Psalm: 34

Jeremiah 6:9–15

Mark 5:1–20

1 Corinthians 6:12–20

It is Sunday—a time to pause and catch our breath on the arduous journey to the cross. Tradition suggests that we break our Lenten fast and celebrate in anticipation of Christ's resurrection. This celebratory pause serves not as a break from the Lenten discipline—as if we simply could not bear another day without sweets or social media. Rather, the pause protects us from excessive introspection and the kind of soul-searching that so easily morphs into unholy narcissism.

Psalm 34 is a helpful guide in drawing our eyes and hearts to God and God's saving action in our lives. It is an unusual psalm in that, unlike many psalms, it is associated with a specific experience in the life of psalmist—most likely 1 Samuel 21. David is fleeing King Saul. He comes to the king of Gath in search of safety, to no avail. Surrounded by potential enemies, David "pretended to be insane in their presence . . . act[ing] like a madman, making marks on the doors of the gate and letting saliva run down his beard" (1 Samuel 21:13). His behavior so disgusts the king that he is sent away instead of being imprisoned or attacked.

David escapes to a cave to hide, but he is still in danger. The journey is not yet over, but he pauses to praise. He declares, "I sought the LORD, and he answered me; he delivered me from all my fears" (Psalm 34:4). There is no pride, no self-congratulatory backslap for David's ingenious escape plan. Rather, the focus is on God and God's power to deliver. God alone can rescue from both the hands of the enemy and the inner turmoil and terror that consume us from the inside out.

As the psalm continues, David's testimony grows into a call to action. *Do you see what God has done for me? Why don't you "taste and see that the LORD is good"* (v. 8)? It is a classic "don't take *my* word for it!" moment. Rather, come and experience this God for yourself, and you will find God to be worthy of trust and devotion.

David's witness stands against the secularism that defined the reign of Saul, who consistently took matters into his own hands rather than waiting on the Lord to deliver. Consumed by a need to preserve his own power, Saul fought to demonstrate his strength and self-sufficiency. Saul's functional atheism threw David's devotion into sharp relief.

As we rest this Sunday, perhaps we might take our cue from David and make space for praise and gratitude. Instead of acquiescing to the functional atheism of our own society that continually pushes us toward idolatrous self-sufficiency and competence as the source of salvation, perhaps we might use this day to re-affix our hearts and minds on the God of our salvation. God delivers. God rescues. God sees and hears. We are not the first or even the primary actors in our own stories; we are respondents to the gracious, loving, saving action of God. Today, taste and see that the Lord is good. May you find rest in the faithful, attentive care of the Lord.

—SDL

REFLECTION & PRACTICE

01 King David's escape from the king of Gath was remarkable. David feigned "madness," appearing to be delusional and crazy. Yet he was aware that the danger he faced was very real. His deliverance was not the result of his clever planning. It was a gift of grace!

- Recall a time when you realized that your self-sufficiency was utterly inadequate, and God stepped in. How do you feel as you reflect on that experience?
- When have your efforts to "manage" your way through a crisis brought you to an even deeper sense of loss and fear? What have you learned about dependence on God as a result?

02 The day of worship in the community of faith can be an opportunity to immerse ourselves in praise and gratitude. In a culture that prizes self-sufficiency and competence, today is a day to step outside that cultural shaping and focus on the source of our redemption.

- How have you seen God's abundant provisions of grace at work in your life? In the life of your home and family? In your church? In the world around you?
- What tangible expression of your gratitude to God can you exercise in your relationships this week? How can you invite others to "taste and see" the grace of God in their lives?

PRAYER

Father, often we forget how utterly dependent we are on your grace and mercy. We have often relied on our own self-sufficiency, our resourcefulness, assuming we can work our own way through the challenges in our lives. We have even assumed we could manage our sin. Forgive us, Lord, for such presumption. Today we will praise you, and we will tell our gratitude with both our lips and our living. You are our only source of redemption. We humbly acknowledge that today, and praise your holy name.

MONDAY

AM Psalm: 80

PM Psalms: 77, 79

Jeremiah 7:1–15

John 7:14–36

Romans 4:1–12

Sometimes it is hard for us to discern what is true and what is not. When a culture is divided and conflicted, truth is often a commodity of relativity. You have "your" truth, and I have "mine." We see this play out across many aspects of life, including politics, business, and, yes, faith.

In our Gospel passage for today, there is a whisper campaign going on. People are afraid to speak out loud, but everyone has an opinion about Jesus. Some say he is a good man. Others are convinced he is a deceiver, a charlatan. They know too much about him. He is too familiar to them. They know where he comes from. *He's no better than any of us—who does he think he is?!*

There are those who are wrestling, not quite sure what to believe. Many people saw the miracle of healing Jesus performed at the Bethesda pool in Jerusalem (John 5:1–11). *When the Messiah comes,* they ask one another, *will he perform more signs than this man?* Yet no one seems ready to take a public stance of fully embracing Jesus as the long-anticipated Messiah. That could be risky because the Jewish leaders have made it clear that Jesus is a threat—a troublemaker. They are looking for a way to arrest

Jesus, but their own uncertainty as to what to do with him is swirling around in their minds.

But Jesus does not leave the issue in limbo. *There is a finite amount of time to make a choice,* he seems to say. *"I am with you for only a short time."*

It is deceptively easy to wallow in indecision when it comes to our journey of faith. In a world of contradictions, of a myriad of voices, of competing demands for our loyalty or belief, we are faced with the hard choice: Are we *really* going to follow Jesus on the Way? Are we going to place *all* our faith in Jesus? Are we prepared to lay aside *every* competing loyalty and build our lives around him?

The Lenten season is an opportunity for us to ask ourselves the hard questions, to probe our own souls. It gives us time and structure to create space for the Spirit of God to speak into our hearts and minds.

When we live attuned to the noise around us, to social media, to the competing news venues that reinforce their own versions of reality, or when we seek distraction through entertainment venues that consume our attention, we easily miss the voice of the Spirit. That voice seeks to check us, to arrest our harried thinking. The Spirit longs to draw us into a fresh encounter with Jesus. The Spirit longs to remind us of the words of Jesus: "My teaching . . . comes from the one who sent me. Anyone who chooses to do the will of God will find out whether my teaching comes from God" (John 7:16, 17). Are you listening?

—JCM

REFLECTION & PRACTICE

01 Truth is no longer *merely* relative; it is *radically* relative. Personal opinion, perception, and experience are the measures of truth.
- What does it mean to commit oneself to the particular person of Jesus in the context of radical relativism?
- In pursuit of truth and obedience to the One who *is* the Truth, how do we guard against reactionary fundamentalism?

02 Fear of inciting the wrath of religious leaders caused many to distance themselves from Jesus, in spite of their spiritual hunger. The risk of being made an outsider was too great.
- What might we risk losing if we followed Jesus, holding nothing back?
- How might a desire to be a comfortable insider bump up against costly discipleship?

03 We are bombarded on all sides by voices proclaiming false gospels—from politicians to marketing teams.
- How might we be more intentional about the voices speaking into our lives?
- What voices might need to be silenced for a season so that we might listen more closely to the voice of the Spirit?

PRAYER

Lord, we confess that we do not always understand your way. Too often we are influenced, even controlled, by voices of the loud and powerful over the quiet voice of the Spirit. Our fear of losing our status or being made an outsider of our group often prevents us from following you without condition. Forgive us, and give us the courage to listen to and obey you alone.

TUESDAY

AM Psalm: 78:1–39

PM Psalm: 78:40–72

Jeremiah 7:21–34

John 7:37–52

Romans 4:13–25

The Jewish Feast of Tabernacles was a joyous celebration. It was originally a celebration of the completion of the harvest, and lasted seven days. The eighth day was one of worship and reflection.

During the seven primary days of the celebration there were processions and lamp lightings. One of the highlights of each day was the march of the high priest to the pool of Siloam to draw water from the pool. Accompanied by worshipers and other religious leaders, the priest entered the temple grounds through the water gate, carrying the pitcher of water from the well. He made his way to the altar, where he poured the water out in celebration of the goodness and protection of God during the forty years of wilderness wandering. It was also poured out in anticipation of the spring rains that would come to water the crops of the land. Water was a precious commodity in Israel. The land depended on the rain for its life and for the crops that were so necessary to survival. Even as they celebrated harvest, they looked forward to the rain so necessary for next year's crops.

As the water was brought to the temple, the crowds sang the Hallel Psalms (113–118) and the joyful phrase from Isaiah 12:3, "With joy you will draw water from the wells of salvation." On the seventh day, when the priest carrying the water from the pool of Siloam approached the altar, he marched around it seven times. The throng sang, and many waved branches they had gathered and bound together. After the priest poured out the water onto the altar, he raised his hands in a symbolic gesture, indicating the completion of the ceremony.

Some commentators suggest it is at that moment, when the ceremony ends, that Jesus speaks in a loud voice, arresting the attention of those in the temple grounds: "Let anyone who is thirsty come to me and drink. Whoever believes in me, as Scripture has said, rivers of living water will flow from within them" (John 7:37–38).

It is a polarizing moment. Some believe Jesus to be a prophet of God. Others say he is the Messiah. Others are still unsure. When you expect God to act in a particular way, it is difficult to imagine anything else is legitimate. When Jesus speaks, we must decide how we will respond. In this case, Jesus's words leave little room for ambivalence. In the act of presenting himself as the one to whom the spiritually thirsty should turn, Jesus confronts the idolatry of allowing a religious practice to become an end in itself. Everything in the worship practices of Israel—everything—is intended to point toward the Messiah, toward Jesus, toward the one who is the final embodiment of everything God intends for the redemption of all things.

The Jewish worshipers—led by the religious establishment—are having a party, but they have failed to recognize the guest of honor! How easily our religious practices become routine and self-satisfying. How necessary to find opportunities to examine our worship, to focus our attention on the guest of honor—the Lord Jesus Christ.

—JCM

REFLECTION & PRACTICE

01 Jesus's intrusion into this ceremony disrupts the expected order. Jesus invites them to shift their attention from the past to the present fulfillment of their hope.

- Think of a time when God disrupted your expectations. How did you respond?
- What can these disruptions teach us about the character of God and the nature of God's work in the world?

02 The invitation of Jesus to the crowds—*Let anyone who is thirsty come to me and drink*—echoes the language of the prophet Isaiah, who—speaking on the Lord's behalf—invited the people of God to repent and turn back to God. Then, they would experience joyful restoration.

- Why would Jesus draw from this particular exilic passage? What parallels might exist?
- The same language is used once again in Revelation 21. In the new creation, God gives water without cost "from the spring of the water of life." What does this repeated theme reveal about the heart of God for us?

03 The people of Israel worshiped the great I AM who provided for them in the wilderness, yet they failed to recognize I AM in their midst.

- What are the things that prevent us from recognizing God at work among us?
- What practices might make us more responsive and attentive to the Spirit's movement?

PRAYER

Lord, we confess that we are often unaware of your presence in our midst. You alone are the source of living water. You alone can heal and nourish us. We repent of our inattention and persistence in self-satisfying religious practices that are more about us than about you, the center of our worship. Satisfy us with the water only you can provide.

WEDNESDAY

AM Psalm: 119:97–120

PM Psalms: 81, 82

Jeremiah 8:18–9:6

John 8:12–20

Romans 5:1–11

The setting for today's Gospel passage is again the Feast of Tabernacles. That occasion was filled with dramatic and symbolic moments that stirred the memories of the faithful. One of the features of the festival was the erection of four large lamp stands. Each evening the stands were lit, and accounts of the event suggest that all of Jerusalem was illuminated by the bright flames of those large lampstands. Those flames symbolized the light of God, recalling the pillar of flame that led and protected Israel during their escape from Egypt and during the forty years of wandering in the wilderness.

When Jesus speaks again to the people his words bring them to a standstill. It might well be when the great lamps are set ablaze—the light filling all the city—that Jesus cries aloud, "I am the light of the world. Whoever follows me will never walk in darkness, but will have the light of life" (John 8:12). For the reader of John's Gospel, there should be an immediate recollection of words found in the opening of the Gospel: "In him was life, and that life was the light of all mankind. The light shines in the darkness, and the darkness has not overcome it" (1:4–5).

Jesus's words bring an immediate rebuke from the Pharisees. From their standpoint this troublemaker is an impostor, and his words are not reliable. They are the experts—the righteous ones—and this man is intruding on their domain.

But Jesus does not need their approval or their endorsement. Knowing who he is, and from whom he comes, Jesus speaks with authority, challenging their assumed superiority with direct and unwavering confidence in his mission.

Doubt and unbelief are not fatal. A genuine struggle to grasp what is true and good often demands deep levels of wrestling with our doubts and uncertainties. What is dangerous is disbelief—*unwillingness* to believe. The ongoing conflict with the Pharisees is not a matter of their wrestling with truth. It is often the willful disregard of the evidence that stands before them. Jesus does not conform to their preconceived ideas about how God works, what a Messiah should do, and how power and dominion should be wielded. Many of them demand an overthrow of Roman power and authority. Jesus offers an alternative kingdom that reigns through peace-making, self-giving love, and care for our enemies. No wonder they refuse to see it—it doesn't *feel* right!

Perhaps the most important part of our Lenten journey is to engage in honest wrestling with our doubts. Are we trying to believe? Or are we determined to resist what does not fit our preconceived idea of what God "should" do?

—*JCM*

REFLECTION & PRACTICE

01 During Israel's wandering in the wilderness, God's presence was manifested as a pillar of light that would ultimately guide Israel toward God's good intentions for them. In what ways is Jesus similar to the pillar of light? How are Jesus and his mission distinctly different from that ancient manifestation of God's presence?

02 Jesus reserves his harshest words for religious insiders who claim to know God. Without hesitation, Jesus declares that the Pharisees do not know him, nor do they know the Father. How are we guilty of practicing the same religious insider-ism of the Pharisees?

03 Jesus is not indignant about hearts that doubt. Rather, he is incensed by hearts that are hard. Doubt is not unfaithful; a spirit actively rebellious toward the Spirit is. How can doubt be a faithful practice? What might it look like to guard against hardness of heart?

PRAYER

Lord, we confess our own spiritual arrogance. We claim to know you yet often live in quiet rebellion. We long to know you truly and to be transformed by the intimacy you desire to cultivate with us. Illuminate our hearts with your light. Cast out the darkness from within us, that we might know you and desire to be known.

THURSDAY

AM Psalms: 42, 43

PM Psalms: 85, 86

Jeremiah 10:11–24

John 8:21–32

Romans 5:12–21

When the winds of change are blowing, confusion, fear, and uncertainty fill the atmosphere. People are on edge. Things once thought stable and predictable seem to teeter on the verge of chaos. Life is uncertain. Of course, life is uncertain in many arenas, be it our health, a job loss, relational crisis, politics, or other things. Sometimes these things accumulate, and we feel a sense of panic or deep anxiety. In such times we need a renewed focus, an effort to orient ourselves toward something that is stable, true, good, and worthy. All of today's readings from Scripture point, in one way or another, to the need to find a place of stability and hope in the midst of chaos and uncertainty.

In the Gospel reading the Jewish leaders are under intense pressure. Even as they celebrate the joyous Feast of Tabernacles, there is an underlying unease—a sense of foreboding—that seems to have permeated everything.

The Jews are under Roman dominion. The Roman Empire has spread over their world, subduing nations, cultures, and religions. As is always the case, "empire" demands loyalty, ritual, and submission. The Jewish people are seeking to live faithfully in the context of an empire that is hostile to their very existence—yet here they are, having to deal with this rebel rabbi who keeps challenging the Jewish leaders' authority and threatening to disrupt the fragile stability of their relationship with Rome. In the face of this anxiety, Jesus speaks to the leaders and the people, standing before them as the source of true stability, hope, and redemption. But they are blinded by their own insecurity and their unwillingness to see Jesus for who he is.

One of the encounters between Jesus and the Jews is a stunning opportunity for them to grasp his true identity. After several exchanges in which they challenge Jesus's authority to do and say the things he has done and said, Jesus responds, "I told you that you would die in your sins; if you do not believe that I am he, you will indeed die in your sins" (John 8:24). In the original language the phrase "I am he" is more emphatic and direct. The words of Jesus were, "If you do not believe that I AM, you will die in your sins."

This is much more than mere banter. The religious leaders are suddenly taken aback. *What on earth is he saying?* That self-description is more than a claim to be *representing* God. It is a claim that standing before them, living with them, and walking among them is the very being of God—the "I AM" of the Exodus, who confronted Moses at the burning bush.

There is perhaps no better time than the Lenten season to get a grip on what is real. In the face of uncertainty, turmoil, pressure, or doubt, look into the face of Jesus. Reorient your heart and mind around the reality of his grace, his love, his presence, his peace. Whatever else may be dominating your life, release it to him—at least for as long as it takes to get a grip on reality—the Christ.

—JCM

REFLECTION & PRACTICE

01 In Scripture, empire is a power standing in direct opposition to God, with the intention of dominating every other power. By definition, empire demands supreme loyalty. Faced with such a violent call to conformity, people of faith often retreat into fundamentalism, legalism, and isolationism.

- What form does empire currently take? We do not live under the rule of Babylon or Rome, but what power structures make the same demands of us today?
- How might we resist the temptations of fundamentalism, legalism, and isolationism? What's the alternative?

02 Even as Jesus speaks difficult words of judgment to those with persistently rebellious hearts, his desire remains the same: to seek and save the lost. If only they would surrender their expectations and preconceived notions to make room for what God is doing! "Judgment" has a negative connotation for most people. How might we understand judgment as an act of mercy and love?

03 Speaking to the believers, Jesus affirms that when they follow him, they are truly disciples. They will know the truth, and the truth will set them free. What might Jesus mean by that? Free from what? Does Jesus offer freedom now, or in the future? Of what do we still need to be freed in order to be faithful disciples of Jesus while living in the world of empires?

PRAYER

Lord, the world continually changes. We often feel powerless as nation feuds with nation and corporations encroach into the very fabric of our daily lives. But we do not want to be a people of fear. Nor do we want to retreat into fundamentalism, legalism, or isolationism. You have called us to be in the world but not of it. Free us from fear. Grant to us soft hearts, open ears, and willing hands that are ready to move in sync with you.

FRIDAY

AM *Psalm: 88*

PM *Psalms: 91, 92*

Jeremiah 11:1–8, 14–20

John 8:33–47

Romans 6:1–11

I am struck today by the despair that is so starkly expressed in Psalm 88, and I think about how familiar Jesus was with the Psalms. As he hung on the cross, his cry of despair is from Psalm 22. He often quoted psalmic phrases, having likely been immersed in those sacred texts from his earliest days.

Psalm 88 is often a companion psalm for folks who struggle through deep depression. It gives voice to the depths of agony that some experience when a betrayal occurs or the death of a loved one intrudes. It can also give voice to the trauma that many in our world go through as a result of war, disease, displacement, and other such events.

In the passage from John, Jesus is facing the intense and growing opposition of the religious leaders of Judaism. Their murderous threats are increasing, and their anger at his persistent challenges to their authority grows by the day.

Jesus stands before them as the very representation of the God they claim as their own. He has offered them light, life, redemption, and instruction. He has healed the sick, given sight to the blind, raised the dead, and announced the in-breaking kingdom of God to people who should have been in ecstasy at his appearing. Instead they have resisted him, criticized him, opposed him, and challenged his every effort to demonstrate the love of the Father.

As tensions in the culture around us escalate, it is not surprising to see a similar response to the people who genuinely represent the love, grace, and compassion of God. Christian communities in some parts of the world are under direct and unrelenting assault, with death threats, destruction of places of worship, and some governments who are threatened by Christian refusal to offer ultimate allegiance to empires.

We can take courage from the unrelenting confidence of Jesus that God is still speaking. "Whoever belongs to God hears what God says," he said to the Jews. In spite of such severe opposition, in the face of their taunts and threats, Jesus persisted in fulfilling his mission. While he was direct and unwavering in his responses to them, his message was clear. He knew who he was, and he was going to fulfill his mission, whatever the cost.

Perhaps one of the most important things we as followers of Jesus can do is to know who we are—and to know *whose* we are. We can then live with the long view in mind. We are the beloved of God. God staked everything on the mission of Jesus to provide redemption and life for us. We are *his!*

So, even when the darkness closes in (Psalm 88:18), and we see no obvious way through, Jesus does not abandon us. He has been there. Thanks be to God!

—JCM

REFLECTION & PRACTICE

01 Psalm 88 is a powerful lament. The writer holds nothing back, describing feelings of loss and abandonment, even perceived abandonment by God. Unlike most lament psalms, this psalm does not shift to remembrance of God's salvation or end with praise. What is the significance of this seemingly unresolved lament? How can this unusual psalm guide us in times of loss, fear, and betrayal?

02 The religious leaders are uninterested in the good Jesus has done, the bodies healed, the minds freed, the broken welcomed. They are more concerned with the disruption of their system and their positions of power.
   - Have you ever been mistreated while doing the good work of God? How did you respond?
   - We are not always the victims; sometimes we are the ones resisting the good work of God because of a perceived threat. Ask the Spirit to reveal, convict, and correct this pattern in you.

03 As Jesus draws nearer to his hour, opposition continues to strengthen. Yet he is not controlled by others' opinions and perceptions. He is free of the need to please, impress, or entertain. How is Jesus able to resist his temptations and persist in mission? Is this same freedom available to us? Why or why not?

PRAYER

Lord, we confess that we do not always live in the truth of our identity as your beloved. In times of fear, distress, and betrayal, we often lash out in anger or withdraw in bitterness. We acknowledge that we have been blind, unable to see what you are doing. We repent of the times when we have inspired fear, caused distress, or betrayed you and others. Convict us, that we might be healed. Do not leave us in our pain—the pain of being wounded or the pain from our sin. Send your Comforter to bind up our wounds and restore us to wholeness.

SATURDAY

AM Psalms: 87, 90

PM Psalm: 136

Jeremiah 13:1–11

John 8:47–59

Romans 6:12–23

If we judge someone too quickly, we may be blinding ourselves to the reality that stands before us. In the Gospel passage for today, the Jews are arguing with Jesus, becoming more and more irritated by his bold persistence and his confidence in God's approval. They hear his words but have dismissed him as a fraud. They throw their most demeaning characterizations at him, calling him a Samaritan and demon-possessed (John 8:48). The further the debate with Jesus develops, the more the Jews display a tragic reality that Jesus makes clear in his responses: once you surrender your mind and values to the "father of lies" (v. 44), the less able you are to discern truth.

The mission of Jesus is to reveal the Father. "I honor my Father," he says. "My Father . . . is the one who glorifies me. I know him . . . and obey his word" (vv. 49b, 54b, 55b). But with every word Jesus speaks, the Jews become angrier, more resistant, and more aggressive. Claiming Abraham as their father, they claim to know him better than Jesus does. When Jesus says that Abraham rejoiced at the very thought of seeing "Jesus's day" (v. 56), the Jews become furious. In doing so they unwittingly reveal their utter unwillingness to receive the magnitude of the revelation God is providing them.

They mock Jesus after he claims that Abraham saw his day "and was glad" (v. 56). Jesus responds with the ultimate revelation of himself: "Before Abraham was, I am" (v. 58). It is not lost on them that Jesus has just made a stunning assertion. He is claiming the divine name—the unutterably holy name; the name by which God, the LORD, revealed God's self to Moses: "I AM."

At that the Jews pick up stones to throw at him, intending to kill him. He escapes, leaving the temple grounds. The one for whom the temple was intended to be a dwelling place is slipping away.

What danger there is in embracing what is not true. What risk there is in trying to walk in the light while holding hands with darkness. The religious leaders—the ones who knew the Law, the Prophets, the Psalms, and the teaching of the elders, those who should have been the first to recognize and embrace the Son of God—were the most blind.

As we prepare our hearts for observing the traumatic events of Holy Week, and as we anticipate the glory of the resurrection, how can we make sure we will recognize the Risen One when he appears? What must we do to assure that we allow him to shape and form us, rather than attempting to shape and form him into our image of what he should be and do?

—JCM

REFLECTION & PRACTICE

01 The religious authorities dismiss Jesus's words by issuing what was, for them, a racial slur—"Samaritan." By casting Jesus as "other," they seek to discredit him. Race-based insults are no longer considered acceptable by the world at large, but especially from Christians. Yet we are still prone to cast someone as "other" to avoid listening and learning. Where have you seen this tendency in your life? Who is the "other" in your life with whom you'd rather not engage?

02 "Are you greater than our father Abraham?" the leaders sarcastically ask, implying that such a thing would be unimaginable.
  • In what ways are our imaginations constricted by how we have experienced God in the past?
  • What might it look like to honor and give thanks for all God has done while maintaining space for the possibility of God acting in a new, unexpected way?

03 The religious leaders ache for God's presence among the people of God, yet their refusal to attend to the new thing God is doing resulted in God-in-the-flesh "slipping away." What attitudes and behaviors drive a wedge between God and ourselves? How might we better attend to what God wants to do in our midst, even if it is contrary to our expectations?

PRAYER

Lord, we shake our heads in disgust at the behavior of the religious leaders—their slander, their idolatry of the past, their lack of humility. Yet we often practice the same things. We discredit the voice of the "other." We elevate the past to the point of idolatry. We pridefully assume we know you best. Forgive us, Lord. Have mercy on us. Humble us and rightly orient us toward you.

FOURTH SUNDAY

IN LENT

AM Psalms: 66, 67

PM Psalms: 19, 46

Jeremiah 14:1–9, 17–22

Mark 8:11–21

Galatians 4:21–5:1

One of the benefits of gathering in worship with the family of faith is the mutual support and encouragement we receive from one another. If you have spent a week working in a setting where faith expression is discouraged, it is a relief to spend time with others who encourage your journey. If you have spent the week embedded in social media—where your anxiety and fear can be amplified by the strident tones of discord and vitriol—you need some peace and quiet. If your home is filled with tension or your relationships are in disarray, the words of Psalm 46:1 might be beneficial: "God is our refuge and strength, an ever-present help in trouble."

In today's Gospel passage, the disciples have just witnessed and participated in one of the feeding miracles of Jesus. It must have been a stunning experience. Having begun with only seven rolls of bread, four thousand people were fed to satisfaction. The disciples clean up the area afterward, filling seven baskets with the leftovers.

Immediately they see Jesus confronted by the Pharisees, demanding that he perform a sign from heaven to validate his authenticity. No wonder Jesus "sighed deeply" (Mark 8:12). He performs no sign.

Once back in the boat, Jesus cautions the disciples to beware the "yeast of the Pharisees" (v. 15). Since they brought only one loaf of bread to the boat (what is that among a group of tired and hungry adults?), they are sure he is scolding them about forgetting to bring more bread.

How very like us! Even when we have seen God at work—such as when the presence of God is manifest in a worship service—when we get back to the workplace, the home, or on social media, our memory fails us. Our fears arise, and our scarcity mentality takes over. We are not enough. We don't have enough of what is needed. There is too much going on in our broken world for us to feel safe or secure.

Jesus pursues those disciples with his questions. He recalls the two feedings they have watched, participated in, and benefited by. He asks them to remember. He challenges them to make some kingdom sense of it all. And they still seem oblivious to the reality that is before them! Who needs more bread when you have Jesus in the boat with you?

It is Sunday. You have opportunity to gather with the people of God and offer your worship to the God who is with us. For this day, lay aside the self-denial and fasting, the compassionate service endeavors, and bask in the presence. Grasp the magnitude of grace. Let the words of Psalm 67:1–2 ring out: "May God be gracious to us and bless us and make his face shine on us—so that your ways may be known on earth, your salvation among all nations."

—JCM

REFLECTION & PRACTICE

01 It is easy to scoff at the religious leaders who demand a "sign from heaven" immediately following the miracle of the seven loaves—a clear reference to the miracle of the manna witnessed by their ancestors. Yet we are often forgetful as well.

- How has God revealed God's self to you in recent days? How has God revealed God's self in your past or the past of your family?
- How might intentional reflection on God's past revelation inform our faith practice now?

02 In spite of witnessing two miracles of abundance, the disciples behave as if the richness of divine provision were a fluke rather than a revelation of the heart and character of God. When has God provided for you in an unexpected and generous way? Why do we so easily fall back into fear of scarcity? What voices and false narratives amplify the lie of scarcity?

03 How does the discipline of corporate worship re-center our lives? How does it better enable us to stand firm against the subtle schemes of enemy?

PRAYER

Lord, we pause on this day to worship you. We set aside all the things that are clamoring for our attention, promising life where none is to be found. We confess that trust and rest do not come easily as we are continually told that we are the source of substance for ourselves. We reject that lie. You are the source, our faithful provider, the restorer of our souls and bodies. You have acted on our behalf in the past, and you will be faithful to do so again. We trust you.

MONDAY

AM Psalm: 89:1–18

PM Psalm: 89:19–52

Jeremiah 16:10–21

John 6:1–15

Romans 7:1–12

In today's Gospel text, the Passover is approaching once again. Families will gather around tables, dipping bitter herbs in salted water and breaking unleavened bread, simultaneously remembering their suffering and God's deliverance. Children will ask the sacred questions: *Why on this night do we eat bread without leaven? Why do we eat the bitter herbs? Why do we eat with our staff in hand and shoes on our feet?* And, once again, parents and grandparents will tell the story of God's saving action. It is the story at the heart of Israel's existence: their deliverance from slavery into the wilderness, where God persistently demonstrated his faithful love and provision through military victories, water from rocks, and the ordinary gift of daily bread by extraordinary means.

The sacramental life of Israel is ordered around this story, yet do the people recognize the story being reenacted before their eyes in John? Do they recognize the hand of God in the roughened hand of Jesus as he passes them a piece of bread, a piece of fish? As the provisions refuse to be depleted, do they recognize the God of their deliverance in their midst? It is the same yet profoundly different. Where the ancestors awoke to jars of worm-infested manna if they dared store a piece overnight, those gathered here in John 6 watch as twelve baskets are filled with the excess—with *sheer abundance.* Nothing will be wasted.

The God of their ancestors is revealing God's very self to them in Jesus. God is not distant, high on a mountain, only to be experienced through a mediator. God is among them, in the flesh, ready to deliver them once again. But this time their deliverance is not from an evil king set on their destruction; Jesus offers deliverance from the powers of sin and death. It is a deliverance that will usher in the healing and restoration of all creation. If only they could have eyes to see the bread for what it is: a sign of God's eternal provision; evidence of God's active presence among them.

How easy it is to stand apart from this story, to have a good-natured chuckle at the slow-to-understand disciples and seemingly oblivious crowds. How do they not see? How do they not recognize God among them? But we must answer the same questions for ourselves. The deliverance of God was initiated by this Jesus, our crucified and resurrected Lord. God is at work among us now. Do we recognize our deliverer? Do we recognize our salvation at hand? We have been given an abundance. We sit surrounded by overflowing baskets of God's saving action. It will not be wasted. May we encounter our saving Lord in the bread, broken for us. May we be filled so we might be poured out for the world.

—*SDL*

REFLECTION & PRACTICE

01 Sacred ritual is an enacted story. A ritual can relate the deep meaning of past sacred deeds or moments by means of the routine of an oft-repeated symbolic activity. What was the significance of the annual celebration of the Passover for the Jewish people? What does it mean for the followers of Jesus to participate in the Lord's Supper?

02 Ritual as remembrance of sacred moments in the past is also intended to be a signpost toward the future. How did Jesus reorient his disciples' understanding of the Jewish Passover? When you think about participating in Communion, what comes to mind? What is the meaning of this meal to you?

03 The disciples did not recognize their salvation at hand, abundant though it was. How have you experienced God's saving action in your life? Why are we often slow to recognize what God is doing in and among us?

PRAYER

Father, our memories are stirred by many things we have experienced, by people we know and love, and by moments of deep meaning. Thank you for the ways you use our memories to prompt us to look to you, to give you praise for your grace and mercy. But thank you as well for those times when our memories produce pain, anguish, or loss, and you step into the memory with your loving assurance that you have not abandoned us, nor will you ever. Help us to recognize you in the midst of our struggle. Help us to cling to hope and to trust your grace and mercy.

TUESDAY

AM Psalms: 97, 99, 100

PM Psalms: 94, 95

Jeremiah 17:19–27

John 6:16–27

Romans 7:13–25

We bought a house in which the bedrooms were constructed without overhead lights. Apparently the builders expected all future homeowners to have a hearty collection of floor lamps! When we first moved in, we only had a few suitcases of possessions, with everything else in storage. Surprisingly, we had no lamps in our suitcases, so every night we hustled to do what needed to be done before night fell. Luckily it was summer. But the sun eventually sets, even in summer, and I found myself stumbling around in the unfamiliar and frustrating darkness with a growing collection of bruises on my shins.

In John's Gospel, darkness is not just the absence of the sun. It is an ongoing metaphor for lack of understanding. In today's passage, the disciples are crossing chaotic waters, engulfed by the thick darkness of a stormy night. They have witnessed the sign of the bread, but they are undoubtedly still "in the dark" about the identity of their teacher. When Jesus appears, walking on the water, the disciples are terrified. The darkness—this state of not knowing who Jesus is or what God is doing in their midst—is unsettling and unfamiliar.

Jesus speaks as God always speaks in a moment of divine revelation: offering comfort and banishing fear, as Jesus makes himself known in a new way: "It is I; don't be afraid" (6:20). If we listen carefully, we hear still more echoes from Exodus, this time from the voice of God in the burning bush: "I AM" (Exodus 3:14). Do they hear it? I AM is in their midst, inviting them to lay aside their fear. Is the light of revelation beginning to peek under the door? Before they can process his presence or words they arrive at their destination, shaken.

The crowds will soon press in again, but Jesus will continue to rebuff their idolatrous pressure. Instead, he will call out their misdirected hunger and invite them to work for the "food that endures to eternal life, which the Son of Man will give you" (John 6:27). Do the crowds hear? Do they see? Or do they too still stumble in the darkness of misunderstanding and wrong-headed expectations?

To both the disciples and the crowds, Jesus is extending a call both to know God more fully and to join God in God's work. It is both revelation and invitation. There are undoubtedly ways in which this text can be understood personally: Jesus coming to us in the stormy darkness and calming our fears, or Jesus challenging us to faithfulness apart from what God does for us. But to think a personal application plumbs the depths of this text is spiritual narcissism. This text is not about us. It is about Jesus making God known among humankind. It is about the God of Abraham, Isaac, and Jacob breaking into the darkness of human sin, confusion, and chaos to set creation free. Do we see it? Do we hear?

—*SDL*

REFLECTION & PRACTICE

01 This is a familiar story, yet it is so easy to miss the essential point of the Gospel writer's purpose in including it. The whole account turns on the words of Jesus in verse 26: "You are looking for me, not because you saw the signs I performed but because you ate the loaves and had your fill."

- Why did Jesus perform the miracle of the feeding of the 5,000? Was human hunger—a legitimate motivation for compassion— the true purpose?
- Have you ever missed the point in what you have expected God to do or what you've asked God to do?

02 When Jesus approaches the boat, walking on the water, the disciples are terrified. His words to them are intended for more than comfort. They are words of identity. What echoes from Exodus do you hear in the words of Jesus? What is the difference between knowing what Jesus can do and knowing who Jesus is?

03 We are comfortable with the image of God comforting us individually during a time of need. We are skeptical of claims that God is breaking into the darkness of creation on a grand scale. How have you witnessed God illuminating darkness in your life? Have you witnessed divine light illuminating darkness on a larger, systemic scale? Why do we naturally lean so heavily toward individualistic interpretations of the text?

PRAYER

Father, we often find ourselves focusing on what you can do for us. As wonderful as that is, help us to begin to focus more on who you are, at the very deepest levels of our understanding. "Tune our hearts to sing your praise." May the light of your presence dispel darkness and fear. May compassion for others begin to lead us to join you in your mission to redeem all of creation for your sake and your glory.

WEDNESDAY

AM Psalms: 101, 109

PM Psalm: 119:121–144

Jeremiah 18:1–11

John 6:27–40

Romans 8:1–11

My son has a tricycle with a special feature. Not only can it be pedaled and steered like a normal tricycle, but it also has a tall handle in the back for parents to push and guide. When he was younger, the tricycle served as a helpful transition between the stroller and him walking completely on his own. He sat happily, hands on handlebars and feet resting on stationary pedals while I pushed and steered. All was well until he realized he too could steer. A calm afternoon walk quickly turned into a wrestling match as he attempted to career his tricycle off the curb with his newfound freedom and I wrangled him back onto the sidewalk.

In today's Gospel passage, we witness a similar struggle. The crowds continue to pull at Jesus, demanding more signs, insisting that he prove himself to be the kind of Messiah they want him to be. But Jesus rights the tricycle again, redirecting their wayward expectations and hopes. He reminds them that Moses was never their savior or provider—God was. And now the ultimate gift of God—the bread of life—is here in him.

"Sir, always give us this bread," they ask (John 6:34). But do they understand that for which they ask? Will they release what they have always known and open themselves up to God's revelation in Jesus? They desire bread, but will they receive the bread of life, or reject him in favor of bread that spoils? Will they allow their hearts, minds, and behaviors to be reshaped to reflect God's in-breaking kingdom?

In Jeremiah 18, the Lord instructs Jeremiah to go down to the potter's house and observe his work. Jeremiah finds the potter shaping clay into a pot, but something is not right. Perhaps the pot is lopsided, or one wall is thicker than another. Whatever the issue, the potter knows the pot cannot fulfill its function as it is, and so the potter "formed it into another pot, shaping it as seemed best to him" (v. 4).

The reshaping is a mercy. It is an act of love, not punitive retribution for disobedience. As the potter reforms the clay, Jesus seeks to reform the imaginations for the people of Israel, that they might recognize him as Lord and Christ and embrace Jesus's invitation into kingdom of God life. So too, the divine Potter longs to reshape us—not because we are worthless as we are but because we are so very valuable and beloved. God's desire is to form us continually into the image of Jesus, that we might be healed and whole.

But will we receive this divine discipline? Will we persist in what Paul in Romans 8 calls living "according to the flesh"? Or will we live according to the Spirit, with our "minds set on what the Spirit desires" (v. 5)? Lest we forget, this Spirit lives in us—the same Spirit who raised Christ from the dead, empowering us to obey. We have all we need to become who we are invited to be if we will submit in trusting obedience to the hand of the Potter.

—*SDL*

REFLECTION & PRACTICE

01 "The Divine Potter longs to reshape us—not because we are worthless
as we are but because we are so very valuable and beloved."

- How does your heart respond to this statement? Do you find it
difficult to fully embrace the idea? Why or why not?
- What do the words of Jesus in the Gospel passage tell us about
God's attitude and bearing toward us?

02 Jesus seems intent on getting the attention of the crowds and his
disciples. The intent is to change their minds, to reorient their
understanding of God's redemptive purposes. How deeply rooted
are we in depending on what we can *do* to please God? What does
Jesus say is the "work" that God requires? How can we move from
depending on our competence to please God to submitting in trusting
obedience to his shaping, loving hands?

PRAYER

*Father, deep within us is the insistent demand that we earn your love and
favor. We need your constant reminder that, contrary to what our culture
may insist is true, your love is unending, reckless, inclusive, and embracing.
We submit ourselves to you in trusting obedience. Shape us into the image of
your Son. We will do the work of believing in your love as expressed in him.
Help us to trust your hands, to rest in your love, and to join you in joyful
service to our neighbors.*

THURSDAY

AM Psalm: 69

PM Psalm: 73

Jeremiah 22:13–23

John 6:41–51

Romans 8:12–27

Grumbling is contagious. One person, or perhaps a small handful of people, can express discontent. An incendiary comment can be made online or an inflammatory article shared. Like a nasty cold, the grumbling spreads. Some limit themselves to snarky comments while others are incited to angry outbursts or even violence. The truth matters less than perception.

In today's Gospel text, the crowds begin to grumble against Jesus. Perhaps the tendency to grumble is hereditary, for the people are doing exactly what their ancestors did in the wilderness: grumbling against God and God's servant. In both cases, the people are dissatisfied with the work of God in their midst. The question of ancient Israel: *how dare God not meet our needs according to our preferences?* Their descendants now ask: *how dare this Jesus claim to be the new manna from heaven? Who does he think he is?* The grumbling reveals nothing about the truth of the situation—namely, Jesus's identity as Messiah. However, it reveals a great deal about the state of the people's hearts: hardened and unyielding. The once attentive, engaged crowd is overtaken by the virus of grumbling. Their posture closes. Their questions take on an accusatory tone.

Contrast the grumbling of John 6 to the groaning in Romans 8. Creation groans "as in the pains of childbirth," in anticipation of the full birth of the kingdom of God (v. 22). Groaning, particularly "as in the pains of childbirth," is vastly different from grumbling. A woman laboring to bring forth a child groans through her tribulation. The pain is often all-consuming. Nothing exists but the suffering—yet it is not purposeless pain. It is suffering that is headed somewhere—namely, to deliverance in the form of birth: new life.

How different from the stubborn posture of grumbling! The grumbler mutters in discontent about the status quo yet stubbornly refuses to welcome the deliverance of God as it comes. The groaner is equally aware of the status quo and the suffering therein but postures herself to engage the suffering, even welcoming it as a harbinger of God's promise of new life. The grumbler will walk away empty-handed. The groaner will be saved by hope. Neither may fully understand the work of God in their midst, but perfect understanding is far less important than trusting obedience.

Trusting obedience does not demand that we deny suffering or pretend we are not wounded, uncertain, or afraid. As Paul reminds us in Romans, we too groan alongside creation as we await our redemption. We call out to God in our hurt, regret, and doubt. In our groaning, the Spirit comes alongside us and expresses our hearts to God.

This Lenten season, may we lay aside our habit of grumbling and instead join with creation in the groaning for redemption, trusting the work of God in and among us.

—*SDL*

REFLECTION & PRACTICE

01 "Grumbling is contagious." In thinking about your own journey or experience, where does the habit of grumbling manifest itself most obviously? How have you experienced the contagion of grumbling?

02 Familiarity can rob us of the ability to see something beyond the expected or the predictable. How are the people influenced by their familiarity with Jesus?

03 "Perfect understanding is far less important than trusting obedience." How do you resonate with this idea? Where might it lead you in your own spiritual journey? Does trusting obedience assure us of perfect understanding? What is the place of "groaning" before God in your spiritual journey?

PRAYER

Father, we are so afraid of uncertainty and a lack of perfect understanding that we hinder your work in shaping us in the image of your Son. As we walk through this Lenten season, as we grapple with our own tendency to grumble when things are not perfectly clear to us, help us learn to trust your unfailing love and faithfulness.

FRIDAY

PM Psalm: 107:33–43

Jeremiah 23:1–8

John 6:52–59

Romans 8:28–39

We have encouraged our children to receive the Eucharist from a very young age. As soon as their little mouths could manage a tiny piece of juice-soaked bread, we brought them to the Table. After a cross-country move, our toddler went through an anxious stage. For a short time, all new things seemed menacing. While the act of receiving Communion was not new, the setting and people were. To prepare her for receiving the familiar sacrament that day in a new place, I talked with her again about the elements: the bread as the body and the juice as the blood. Her eyes widened in toddler horror. "Blood?! I no want it!"

Imagine the similar faces of the crowd in John as Jesus instructs the people to eat his flesh and drink his blood in order to have life. Undoubtedly, his words are shocking and offensive. Like my daughter, their eyes surely widen and their mouths twist in disgust and confusion. *What is this strange teaching?* Not even the Romans—the violent enemy of the Jewish people—would participate in so vile a practice as *cannibalism*.

But Jesus is speaking of a different reality. "My flesh is real food and my blood is real drink" (John 6:55). What Jesus offers nourishes us far beyond satisfying the rumblings of our stomachs. It nourishes us at the core of our being. Jesus reminds the crowd of the gift of manna to ancient Israel. The bread given from heaven fed their bodies and sustained their very beings because it reminded them of God's presence and provision. But as wonderful as the gift of manna was, it was still only bread; it was not bread of the age to come. Only by feasting on the flesh and blood of Christ—his self, given for the world—can we enter into the life of the age to come.

It is not mere metaphor. Receiving his flesh and blood joins us with the triune God in a mysterious and unseen—but nonetheless *real*—way. We are united with Christ's death, by which he gave himself over for the sake of the world, as well as his resurrection, by which he freed us from sin and death. United with him, we are not only nourished by his gift but also invited to embody his way of self-giving. We too give ourselves for the sake of the world. It will not be our lives that nourish and save the world; it will be Christ in us. We are the vessel; Christ is the food. Many give their lives in service to others, and often do good work. But it is not work that will last into the age to come. Only work that is fueled by the flesh and blood of Christ will bring about transformation that lasts into eternity. We are invited both to consume and distribute this flesh and blood that nourish us into the coming kingdom.

—SDL

REFLECTION & PRACTICE

01 Jesus uses a stunning metaphor when speaking to the Jews in the synagogue in Capernaum. But it is so much more than a metaphor. It speaks of a profound spiritual reality that reaches into the most tangible expressions of our lives. As you think about Jesus's reference to eating his flesh and drinking his blood, what do you think he is asking of us? What does this imply about our relationship with him?

02 Our misinterpretation of this metaphor can make it seem as if a relationship with the triune God is somehow less than "real." It can tempt us to separate the spiritual from the practical tangibility of the rest of our lives. How can the words of Jesus and the suffering, death, and resurrection of Jesus be translated into the way we live our lives? How may the self-giving of Jesus be lived out in our relationships?

PRAYER

Father, we are stunned by the words of Jesus in our passage today. It seems at first glance to be awkward and, perhaps, a bit embarrassing to talk about with other people. Yet, in the very act of embracing the complexity of this metaphor, we find ourselves gripped by your love and faithfulness. You enable us, by our participation in the body and blood of Christ, to receive your grace and mercy. In doing so, you transform us to live the same self-sacrificing love that so characterized your Son. Thank you for providing us so simple a moment as to drink a small portion of the fruit of the vine and to eat a tiny morsel of bread. As we do so, may we be struck by the realization that this is the measure of your love for us and for all. May we live in such ways that your presence in our lives becomes a tangible expression of your love for all.

SATURDAY

AM Psalms: 102, 108

PM Psalm: 33

Jeremiah 23:9-15

John 6:60–71

Romans 9:1–18

When I was a child, my parents frequently said to me, "Listen and obey!" Their message was clear. *Don't just hear my words. Do what they say.* Now that I am a mother to young children, I find myself saying the same thing. I do not want my children to merely hear and understand my words to them. I want them to *enact* them so they can experience the good things that I intend for them.

We finally come to the end of the very long chapter in John 6. Jesus's followers are unsettled by what they have heard and declare, "This is a hard teaching. Who can accept it?" (v. 60). The word translated as "accept" comes from the verb *akouō*, a weighty term that carries the implication of both listening *and* obeying. These people have heard and experienced the Word of God—Jesus—but they have not obeyed, and will not. They are scandalized, and they scatter.

Jesus looks at the Twelve who are still standing next to him silently. Are they also scandalized? Will they scatter and go about their lives, thinking back on their time with Jesus with confusion and shame?

Peter speaks for the group: "Lord, to whom shall we go? You have the words of eternal life" (v. 68).

The writer of John's Gospel references eternal life frequently. Formed as we are by images of floating on clouds and walking streets of gold in a far off *somewhere*, we might miss what Peter—and this Gospel at large—is declaring. Eternal life refers not to some disembodied existence in an alternative reality. The original text and context are better understood as the *life of the age to come*. Life of the age to come is kingdom-of-God life, and it begins now. Not someday. In spite of all the confusion, all the teachings the disciples almost certainly do not comprehend, they are coming to understand this: Jesus is speaking and acting in such a way that is bringing the kingdom of God into their very midst. They are beginning to understand, and will continue to grow in the knowledge, that the kingdom of God does not come by swords or power or human virtue. It comes through the Word of God.

Our very life, in this moment, can be transformed by that kingdom as we *akouō*—listen and obey. Many followers hear the words of Jesus but are not transformed by them. We can read Scripture daily, join studies, and listen to countless sermons. But only when we submit in trusting obedience to the way of the kingdom of God are we changed from mere hearers of the word to *doers*. Our doing does not gain us entrance into the life of the age to come. Rather, our doing is the fruit of living toward the life of the age to come.

—*SDL*

REFLECTION & PRACTICE

01 It is obvious by this time in John's Gospel that Jesus has quite an entourage, but it is also obvious that those who make up this rag-tag group are not all of one mind. What is the difference between being a *follower* of Jesus and being a *disciple* of Jesus? What does it mean for us to listen *and* obey?

02 Jesus has spoken often about eternal life. We often speak of it as well.
   • What does it mean for us to have eternal life?
   • How do you give concrete expression to eternal life?

03 Jesus said that the words he spoke were "full of the Spirit and life."
   • What did Jesus mean when he said that?
   • How do we appropriate the Spirit and the life the Spirit brings?

PRAYER

Father, we find ourselves in familiar company in the Gospel passage for today. The crowds were there, but they were not all of one mind. There were some who merely followed and others who threw themselves fully into acknowledging Jesus as the holy one of God. May we be among those who genuinely listen and obey. Help us to overcome our own reticence and our self-sufficiency. Help us to take the conscious and necessary steps to believe, trust, and obey.

FIFTH SUNDAY

IN LENT

AM Psalm: 118

PM Psalm: 145

Jeremiah 23:16–32

Mark 8:31–9:1

1 Corinthians 9:19–27

"Take up your cross" is one of those phrases that has become so familiar it has almost entirely lost its meaning. Even people who are not followers of Jesus know the phrase and even often say, "It's my cross to bear." Taking up and bearing one's cross has almost become equivalent to enduring hard things. Let's be clear: that is not your cross. Difficult things in our lives—like bad bosses, chronic illness, or the like—are thorns (see 2 Corinthians 12). Sometimes God relieves them and sometimes he doesn't, choosing instead to use them as instruments of sanctification in our lives.

Taking up our cross is an entirely different matter. For Jesus to take up his cross was to embrace public shame and perceived failure in the eyes of both the Jewish people and the powerful Romans. To take up his cross was to resist the powers at work in the world. It was to resist their *vision* of the world but also to resist their way of *imposing* that vision on the world through violence and coercion. To take up his cross meant that Jesus was aligning himself not only with the *will* of God but also with the *way* of God. God's will done in God's way—namely, through self-sacrifice for the redemption of creation, not through power and violence. The cross is the eternal "no" of God to revenge, violence, power games, and cycles of retribution.

It is this cross that we are called, by Jesus himself, to take up. Too often we mistakenly look at the life of Jesus, at the cross, and at the empty tomb as being all about us—a religious good to consume in order to secure our eternal destinies. Our distorted, self-centered view of salvation goes no further than our own hearts, a pocket-sized Messiah.

This is not the kingdom of God declared in word and deed by Jesus. This is not the gospel taught and embodied by Jesus. The gospel is God come down, God among us, God for us, God emptying God's self out on behalf of all of creation. It is the gospel of a suffering God who endures shame and violence in order to turn it on its head and free us from the chains of darkness. And it is a gospel that beckons us, not only to partake of the blessings of God's work in Jesus but also to enact that same kingdom work. God's will (forgiveness, restoration, redemption), done in God's way (rejecting violence, power and coercion).

God's will done in God's way. May it be so in and among us.

—SDL

REFLECTION & PRACTICE

01 Rev. Lobdell suggests there is a difference between a cross and a thorn. How do you understand that distinction? How has that distinction been experienced in your own life?

02 Jesus has been persistent in telling his disciples that he will face suffering, rejection, persecution, and death. Beyond the idea of his own physical death on a cross, what else does Jesus imply by calling on his disciples to take up their cross? What does Jesus mean when he says we must deny ourselves, take up our cross, and follow him?

03 "The Gospel is God come down, God among us, God for us, God emptying God's self out on behalf of all of creation." How is this a pattern for us in our journey with Christ? What does it mean for you to do God's will in God's way?

PRAYER

Father, we prefer our religion served on a silver platter, before adoring crowds. But your Son endured shame, suffering, and death in order to purchase for us so much more than a self-oriented, self-serving religious "experience." Help us follow Jesus passionately, intimately, and faithfully. May we not seek to equate our thorns with his cross. Rather, may we live so like Jesus that our lives become reflections of his self-giving love for all of creation.

MONDAY

AM Psalm: 31

PM Psalm: 35

Jeremiah 24:1–10

John 9:1–17

Romans 9:19–33

    The question of why bad things happen is a recurring and all-consuming one, especially when it is the righteous who suffer. The disciples of Jesus—seeing a man who was blind from birth—ask Jesus this very question. In their asking they couch the question in the form we so often bear in the back of our minds when we see suffering: "Who sinned, this man or his parents?" (John 9:2). It is so easy to assume a connection between the suffering of another—their misfortune, their ill health, the devastation of natural disaster—and what they must have done to "deserve" this. When we make that connection, we fail to recognize the reality of life in a broken world. Life does not come with a guarantee of safety and good fortune. Following Christ is not a ticket to paradise in this world as it now exists. Storms come. Health crises arise. Auto accidents occur. King David gives voice to that reality in Psalm 31:10: "My life is consumed by anguish and my years by groaning; my strength fails because of my affliction, and my bones grow weak."

    The response of Jesus to the disciples' question in John 9 can be misconstrued. It almost sounds as if he is saying it happened as part of God's plan. What may be better understood is that God can work in spite of calamity. God is present in the midst of anguish. For the believer, our greatest assurance is that we are not abandoned. God is indeed with us. He is our Emmanuel. But that does not necessarily assure us that we will avoid the losses of life, or that—when they occur—God was somehow absent or not paying attention. It *does* mean that God's grace is sufficient.

For the one who faces the burden of depression, often unrelenting and reoccurring, the hope is that God will sustain and remain close. While medicine and treatment are often effective in helping us through depression and into relief and restoration to hope, there are times when our bodies do not cooperate with the grace of God or the efforts of physicians. For those folks, the compassionate and supportive presence of friends and loved ones through the valley of depression is a critically necessary part of the journey—part of the lived-out grace of God.

Certainly, there are indeed consequences for sin. But not all loss is the consequence of sin. And even when God comes through in redeeming and restoring, as God so often does, that does not mean the journey will then become easy. The blind man was given sight, but with sight came conflict, judgment, and exclusion.

Lent is a season for self-examination, not only for the purpose of directing us toward deeper reliance on the grace and goodness of God, but perhaps also for grace to endure the consequences that might occur when God does indeed answer prayer!

—JCM

REFLECTION & PRACTICE

01 Why do we often feel the need to determine the cause and purpose of suffering? What are some of the answers we tend to rely on most heavily?

02 Christians often engage in debate around the question of suffering, asking whether God causes or allows suffering. Are either of these options in keeping with God's character? Why or why not? If we take the fallenness of creation—as well as God's unrelenting love for creation—seriously, how might our answer to the question of suffering change?

03 Regardless of the cause of suffering, God is present with us in the midst of it. How have you experienced God as Emmanuel in the midst of suffering? As disciples of Jesus, how might we practice faithful presence with those who suffer?

PRAYER

Lord, the weight of suffering is burdensome. Our entire beings, spirits, and bodies tell us that suffering is contrary to your design. We confess that we often turn to idolatrous, unfair, and even abusive explanations for suffering. We seek to justify ourselves but also to guard ourselves against the unspoken fear that you might be silent in the face of suffering. Help us to face suffering with courage in the knowledge that new creation is on the way and that, in this time of tension, you are present—closer than breath.

TUESDAY

AM Psalms: 121, 122, 123

PM Psalms: 124, 125, 126

Jeremiah 25:8–17

John 9:18–41

Romans 10:1–13

We prefer to identify good and evil in behavioral and moral categories so we can spot sin from a distance! We also think it helps us identify who is in and who is out. If only it were actually that simple.

In the story of the healing of the man born blind in John 9 we find the disciples asking Jesus to help them understand what happened in this man's life. *Who sinned? What must they have done for this tragedy to result?* An uncomfortable implication of their question is the assumption that, if the man's parents were Law-observing Jews, then what could *he* possibly have done to be born blind?

Such questions will never solve the dilemma. Sin is so much more than this behavior or that. Certainly there are boundaries and practices that are detestable—"unlawful"—that defy the moral categories of right and wrong. In fact, the plight of Judah in today's Jeremiah passage makes abundantly clear the consequences for sinful practices: "'But you did not listen to me,' declares the LORD, 'and you have aroused my anger with what your hands have made, and you have brought harm to yourselves'" (25:7).

But in John 9 there is a much larger issue that is easily overlooked. When Jesus makes the mud from spittle and places it on the blind man's eyes, he kneads the mud. He mixes it with his fingers. According to the teaching of the elders, such work as kneading dough—using the hands and fingers to mix flour and water—is prohibited work on the Sabbath. In the eyes of the Pharisees, Jesus is a sinner because he has broken the Law by mixing the dust and saliva with his fingers. In the extended description of the Pharisees' investigation of the healing, their accusations are fierce and persistent. The parents of the man are summoned for testimony. The man who was healed is interrogated. Every effort is made to discredit the miracle.

But the sin that dominates the entire episode has nothing to do with Jesus breaking Sabbath. In the Gospel of John, there is a more foundational aspect to sin. It is not that moral categories do not exist. It is that, when Jesus—Emmanuel, the Son of God—shows up, walks among the people, teaches in the synagogues, and heals, the Pharisees refuse to recognize him. For John, a greater sin than breaking the Sabbath is rejecting Jesus. Unbelief is fatal. Behavior is symptomatic rather than causal. The blind man can now see, but the Pharisees, in their fierce rejection of Jesus, have revealed the depth of their blindness.

"He came to that which was his own, but his own did not receive him" (John 1:11).

The next opportunity we have to come before God in confession, where should we begin?

—JCM

REFLECTION & PRACTICE

01 The religious leaders are so consumed by their desire to maintain the clear boundaries that define God's chosen people that they are blind to God's kingdom breaking in among them. Do we ever become consumed by external indicators of faithfulness? How do we discern between idolatrous fixation and a healthy concern for moral living?

02 In the story, the parents refuse to engage in the conversation surrounding their son's healing because they are afraid of the Pharisees, who have been threatening to expel from the synagogue any Jews who believe in Jesus as the Messiah. Do we ever weaponize inclusion? To what end? What impact might fear of exclusion have on a faith community?

03 Dr. Middendorf says in this chapter, "Behavior is symptomatic rather than causal."
- Do you agree or disagree? Why?
- What might our behavior be symptomatic of?
- Pause and reflect on the patterns in your life and ask the Spirit to open your eyes to veiled motivations.

PRAYER

Lord, we confess that we are often blind to your work among us. We acknowledge that we too have weaponized inclusion in misguided attempts to protect our idols. We confess that often we would rather stand on the sidelines in silence to protect our position than risk our place by speaking the truth on behalf of others. We admit we are the ones in need of healing and forgiveness. Restore us, Lord, that we might see more clearly and walk more faithfully.

WEDNESDAY

AM Psalm: 119:145–176

PM Psalms: 128, 129, 130

Jeremiah 25:30–38

John 10:1–18

Romans 10:14–21

We live in a world where conditional love is the norm. The love we receive is conditioned on our worthiness, our appeal, or our appearance. We attempt to mask our imperfections in order that we may be accepted and loved. This conditional understanding of love has also crept into our understanding of the Christian journey. While we tout grace as the only basis for our redemption, many of us fret and worry deep inside that somehow we are not worthy or do not measure up. So we spend much of our lives in uncertainty, seeking to prove ourselves worthy by our behavior, by costly sacrifice, or by rigorous discipline. Such efforts sometimes cause us to so despair of ever reaching a state of acceptance before God that we fear we must walk away from faith for our own mental and emotional survival.

Performance-based Christianity is oppressive. That is not to say there are no consequences to sin, but there is a marked difference between obstinate refusal to believe God and obey, and fearful uncertainty about whether we are worthy of God's love. Jeremiah 25:30–38 makes clear that such obstinate disbelief and blatant disobedience will face certain judgment. But John 10:1–18 makes equally clear that the posture of God toward broken humanity is one of passionate, pursuing love.

The appeal that Jesus makes in these verses is a mystery to the Pharisees. That should not be surprising to us. They resist and oppose everything he says and does. They see what everyone else sees, hear what others hear, and are close enough to see miracles performed. The sick are healed, the hungry fed, and the blind receive sight. The more the Pharisees see and hear, the less they understand. In verse 6 the Gospel writer makes a poignant observation: "Jesus used this figure of speech, but the Pharisees did not understand what we was telling them."

Jesus is the perfect revelation of the Father. In Jesus we see the bearing of God toward us. What we see is not judgment and condemnation. Rather, we see Jesus embodying the always-reaching love of God, offering grace, forgiveness, and freedom from guilt and shame. We see the image of the Shepherd who intimately knows his sheep, cares for them, protects them, reaches out to them, and leads them. He teaches them and lays down his life for them.

For the Pharisees this seems scandalous. Many of them say he is demon-possessed and raving mad. To some today, the images Jesus uses in these eighteen verses in the Gospel of John seem incongruous with what we have heard or experienced in our interaction with some manifestations of the church. Perhaps only during Lent can we immerse ourselves in a new understanding of what Jesus has come to do. For many, this is a startling new vision of God. It could be utterly reorienting and liberating. Let it soak in. It could change you!

—JCM

REFLECTION & PRACTICE

01 It is often said, "God loves everyone, but . . ."
- What conditions or boundaries do we often attach to this statement?
- Why are we uncomfortable letting God's unconditional love stand alone?

02 Contrast "performance-based Christianity" and a life marked by obedience to God. How might motives differ between the two perspectives? What fruit might come from these distinct postures?

03 Jesus contrasts the image of the good shepherd with a hired hand. What are the differences between the two roles—not only in function but also in motive and purpose? Based on those differences, what might it look like to live in the knowledge that Jesus is the Good Shepherd, not a hired hand?

PRAYER

Lord, we confess our struggle to trust your love as unconditional, for ourselves and for others. In a world that measures our worth by our accomplishments, competencies, and prestige, we are unsettled by the divine economy of love: abundant and free. Disentangle the lies that keep us bound in performance-based religion. May we come to trust you as the Good Shepherd, and may that trust transform us from the inside out.

THURSDAY

AM Psalms: 131, 132, 133

PM Psalms: 140, 142

Jeremiah 26:1–16

John 10:19–42

Romans 11:1–12

A recurring theme in the tenth chapter of the Gospel of John is the ability of the sheep to recognize the voice of their shepherd. In a blunt assessment of the Jews who are challenging him, Jesus says to them that they "do not believe because you are not my sheep" (v. 26).

One of the endearing things early on about the woman who became my wife was her voice. Early in our relationship her voice became important to me. I came to recognize it as I had never recognized another voice. For several years my assignment involved extensive global travel. But one of the commitments I made to Susan was the promise that, unless it was impossible, I would find some way to communicate with her every day I was away from home. Sometimes it was through social media or text. But, whenever possible, I made a phone call. I wanted to hear her voice. And whatever the situation—whether the call was clear or filled with static or background noise—I could recognize her voice. It was a priceless gift to be able to hear her voice.

Jesus describes the relationship of the shepherd and the sheep with great insight. The sheep know the voice of the shepherd. They will not follow the voice of another. One of the great challenges of discipleship is to learn to discern the voice of the Shepherd. That does not happen easily or quickly. We do have Scripture, and through it God speaks to us. We also have the voice of faithful Christian friends and family members, and often the Spirit of God speaks to us through them too. But it is necessary for us to learn to hear the voice of the Shepherd for ourselves. As we read Scripture, we begin to learn how and why the Spirit speaks to us. It is not for our own benefit, as a means to get what we want. It is the way we learn to listen to and recognize the voice of Jesus. The better we know the Shepherd, the more we learn to recognize the voice of the Shepherd.

Another way we get to know the voice of the Shepherd is through prayer. Prayer involves more than telling God what we want. We learn to spend time in quiet and intentional listening in the deep inner recesses of the heart and mind. As we listen, we recognize the voice of the Shepherd when what we hear is consistent with what Scripture says about the character and the virtues of Jesus.

The Lenten journey provides us insight into the character of the Shepherd. Perhaps the best part of the journey could be learning to recognize the voice of the Shepherd. The Shepherd is not silent. The voice is speaking, even when we are not listening well. Set aside some time during this journey to stop—even for a few minutes—and listen. Tune out the static and the background noise and simply listen. You will fall in love with the voice.

—JCM

REFLECTION & PRACTICE

01 Whose voice do you recognize without fail? How did you become so attuned to that person's voice?

02 Sheep recognize the voice of their shepherd.
  - When have you heard the voice of the Shepherd? What did the Lord use to communicate with you?
  - How do you nurture discernment to recognize that voice consistently?
  - What safeguards might prevent us from confusing our own desires or the many competing voices around us with the voice of the Shepherd?

03 Sheep not only recognize the voice of their shepherd; they will not follow the voice of another. It does us no good to recognize the voice of our Shepherd if we do not follow him.
  - How do we cultivate trust in our Shepherd? How might this trust strengthen our ability (and willingness!) to obey?
  - What might it look like to practice heeding the voice of the Shepherd in community instead of exclusively in isolation?

PRAYER

Lord, we confess that we are not always good listeners. Sometimes we are distracted by other voices, and other times we rebelliously stop our ears against your voice. Yet you persist. You continue to call us by name. Attune our ears to your voice. In trust, may we heed your voice and follow where you lead.

FRIDAY

AM *Psalm: 22*

PM *Psalms: 141, 143*

Jeremiah 29:1, 4–13

John 11:1–27

Romans 11:13–24

The account of the sickness and death of Lazarus seems appropriate for the Lenten journey. This season is a somber one in many ways. We search our hearts, we participate in self-denial and fasting. We seek to serve the less fortunate, which reminds us of the brokenness of our culture and our world.

The story is difficult because of Jesus's delay in responding to the urgent pleas of Mary and Martha, the sisters of Lazarus. These people are close friends of Jesus. He has spent time in their home and eaten at their table. Mary is the one, says John, who anointed Jesus with oil and wiped his feet with her hair. This is not a casual relationship. And the plea is pointed: "The one you love is sick" (John 11:3).

That Jesus loves these three people is made clear in the passage. That he stays where he is for two more days is puzzling. When he does go, the disciples are hesitant. Going back to Judea will be risky. Threats to Jesus's life have been made, and the disciples know that the threats inevitably extend to them, his followers.

There are multiple levels of interaction and meaning in this story, but there is a clarifying focus that is essential to our Lenten journey: death has come. Lazarus, the one Jesus loves, has died in spite of the fervent pleas of his sisters. Jesus—the one they knew would've been capable of healing their brother—arrives four days after the sickness has taken its final toll. "If you had been here . . ." (v. 21).

It is fascinating that Martha does not waver in her confidence that God will give to Jesus whatever Jesus asks. But Jesus is taking her to a deeper realization than she can imagine. "Your brother will rise again" (v. 23).

That much she knows, and expresses with heartfelt certainty: "I know he will rise again in the resurrection at the last day" (v. 24).

In the Apostles' Creed we confidently affirm our belief in "the resurrection of the dead and the life everlasting." It is a wonderful affirmation we cling to with hope and anticipation. But Jesus will not leave Martha with that affirmation. Belief in the resurrection, as assuring as that may be, is not sufficient. Jesus takes Martha to the Person on which belief in the resurrection is grounded. This is the point of it all. Physical death is real, but it is not final. Resurrection life is available, and it begins now. Our hope is not in a belief. It is a Person. "Jesus said to her, 'I AM the resurrection and the life. The one who believes in me will live, even though they die; and whoever lives by believing in me will never die. Do you believe this?'" (vv. 25–26).

Do *you* believe this? Do you *really* believe this?

—JCM

REFLECTION & PRACTICE

01 Jesus does not immediately respond to the request of Mary and
Martha. Have you ever felt that God was silent or unresponsive? How
did you navigate that period of uncertainty?

02 Martha acknowledges her faith in the future resurrection, but it is clear
that she longs for divine intervention *now,* not just *someday.* How have
you experienced the tension between our future hope and the desire
for restoration and healing now?

03 "Resurrection life is available, and it begins now." What does it mean
to experience resurrection life *now*? When have you experienced
resurrection life? How did you identify resurrection power at work?

PRAYER

*Lord, we confess that, like Mary and Martha, we are frustrated and
disappointed when you do not intervene in the way and on the timetable
we desire. We look forward to new creation with hope, yet we hunger for
restoration and redemption now. We long for your resurrecting Spirit to come
and revive what seems beyond hope in and around us. May we cast our full
trust not upon a doctrine but upon your shoulders—our resurrection and life.*

SATURDAY

AM Psalms: 137, 144

PM Psalms: 42, 43

Jeremiah 31:27–34

John 11:28–44

Romans 11:25–36

Sometimes we are sure that if God knew what we know about a situation, then God would act the way we expect God should act. In chapters 9–11 of Romans, Paul genuinely wrestles with the spiritual destiny of the Jews—the people of God. As the "apostle to the gentiles," Paul is convinced that the kingdom of Christ is open to everyone. But as a son of Israel, formerly known as Saul, he devoted his early life to learning the story of Israel. He was originally a fierce opponent of the "Jesus movement." But on a mission to Damascus to further disrupt this sect, he had an encounter with the resurrected Jesus, and everything changed. Now, some years later, Paul is writing to the church in Rome, assuring them that gentiles are welcomed into the kingdom of Christ on the basis of grace, through their faith in Jesus—the crucified and risen Lord. They did not have to go through the Jewish rituals to become the people of God; instead, they were accepted through the grace of God.

But Paul also wants the Romans to know that the Jews—those who have been the exclusive people of God up until now, the people through whom all the law and the prophets came—are also welcomed into the kingdom of Christ. But, instead of their welcome being a product of their ancestry as it was in the past, they are now welcomed on the same basis as the gentiles: by grace, through faith. This news has been welcomed by the gentiles, but the Jews—even many who already believe in Jesus as the Messiah—are convinced that being Jewish is *essential*. It just doesn't seem right for it to be any other way.

When Jesus arrived in Bethany, Lazarus had been dead for four days. In his encounter with Martha and Mary he heard each of them say to him, "Lord, if you had been here my brother would not have died." Even the mourners who were gathered around the sisters raised the question. Why didn't Jesus do what we expected him to do?

The risk we all face is the tendency to squeeze God into our boxes, to expect God to act on our behalf in ways that conform to our expectations. But Paul grasps the magnitude of God's wisdom and God's love. In the doxology at the end of Romans 11, Paul sings his praise to a God who is not confined to our boxes, nor required to fulfill our expectations as to how God should carry out the mission of redemption. As we move toward Palm Sunday, perhaps it is time to sing: "Oh, the depth of the riches of the wisdom and knowledge of God! How unsearchable his judgments, and his paths beyond tracing out! 'Who has known the mind of the Lord? Or who has been his counselor? Who has ever given to God, that God should repay them?' For from him and through him and for him are all things. To him be the glory forever! Amen" (Romans 11:33–36).

—JCM

REFLECTION & PRACTICE

01 Jesus responded to Mary and Martha's need but not in the way or in the time frame they desired. How have you experienced God responding to your need differently than you desired or expected? In retrospect, do you recognize any unforeseen acts of divine grace?

02 Claiming unshakable certainty in how and when God will act is a dangerous practice bordering on idolatry. How does this kind of certainty inhibit our ability to perceive God's work in and around us? What role might humility and submission play in protecting us against this form of idolatry?

03 Paul's doxology in Romans 11 invites us to worship God as both revealed yet also not fully comprehensible to us. What might it look like to practice radical trust in this God whose wisdom and knowledge go beyond human imagination? How might our lives be marked by the affirmation that *all things* are from God, through God, and for God?

PRAYER

Lord, we confess our tendency to attempt to contain you in the small boxes of our understanding. We often prefer a god we can define without remainder. Yet you show yourself to be worthy of our trust, time and again. Teach us to release our idolatrous expectations, that we might be open to experience you as you truly are.

PALM SUNDAY

AM Psalms: 24, 29

PM Psalm: 103

AM Zechariah: 9:9–12

PM Zechariah: 12:9–13:9

Matthew 21:12–17

1 Timothy 6:12–16

The Palm Sunday dilemma plagues every pastor. Do we celebrate the triumphal entry of Jesus into Jerusalem to the acclaim of the crowd? Or—since some churches do not host Holy Week services later in the week (and, even of those who do, attendance is much lower than on Sundays)—do we face the impending agony of the arrest and trial, the brutal torture, and the crucifixion? To further complicate the issue, Matthew's Gospel places the triumphal entry into Jerusalem and the cleansing of the temple in close connection to one another, both near the end of Jesus's life. John's Gospel, on the other hand, places the cleansing of the temple early in the life of Jesus, disconnected from the triumphal entry. There is no "right" answer, so many pastors choose to alternate each year. They bring their people through the celebration of Jesus as Lord one year and lead them to see Jesus as the Suffering Servant the next.

In today's Lenten Gospel reading, we find Jesus in the temple, overturning "the tables of the money changers and the benches of those selling doves" (Matthew 21:12). He was just welcomed into the city of

Jerusalem, acclaimed as the Son of David, "he who comes in the name of the Lord!" (v 9). Matthew's account finds him moving from acclaim into the temple. It seems only right! The Temple was intended to be the meeting place of God and creation. At the heart of the temple is the Holy of Holies, the place where God is "seated." It is the sacred inner space where only the high priest can enter, and only once a year. He goes in, representing the worshiping congregation gathered at the temple. It is the place to which every Jew comes to worship, to offer sacrifices, and to acknowledge Israel's God. But at its best, God is still at a distance.

When Jesus enters the temple on this momentous day, things shift dramatically. "'It is written,' he said to them, '"My house will be called a house of prayer," but you are making it a "den of robbers"'" (v. 13). What the temple is intended to be, it is no longer. But then the blind and the lame come to Jesus "at the temple," and he heals them (v. 14). In a stunning moment of revelation, the meeting place of God and creation, of God and humanity, has radically changed. Now the meeting place of God is Jesus—the new temple. Now, access to God is no longer mediated through priests and sacrifices, with the "seat" of God hidden behind thick curtains. God shows up in the flesh. Jesus becomes the dwelling place of God, the very presence of God among the people.

Psalm 29 is a majestic description of the presence of God described in terms of storms and earthquakes. The glory of God is revealed in the power of storms that break the cedars. The sound of thunder is likened to the voice of God. The oaks are twisted, and the seas roar. I have experienced hurricanes, tornadoes, and violent thunderstorms. I have been in awe of the power of nature. For the writer of Psalm 29, such awesome moments are reminders of the power, the majesty, and the presence of God.

The purpose of the temple has been thwarted by abusive, exploitative practices, like the buying and selling of animals and currency exchange in what should be a place of prayer and worship. But when Jesus, the meeting place of God and humankind, appears in the temple, all the intrusion is disrupted. In the aftermath, the glory of God is revealed in the healing of the lame and the giving of sight to the blind. I imagine it thundered in that place! As you go to worship this morning, be on the lookout. Listen carefully. It just might thunder!

—JCM

REFLECTION & PRACTICE

01 In Matthew's account, the triumphal entry and the cleansing of the temple are closely intertwined. The Son of David has come not to embrace the power of the religious system but to reorient it entirely.
- What does Jesus's choice to immediately cleanse the temple following his dramatic entry into Jerusalem reveal about how he intends to steward power?
- Does our stewardship of power more closely resemble the religious leaders' stewardship or that of Jesus?

02 The buying and selling in the courts impacts the most vulnerable worshipers: non-Jewish God fearers who are coming to pray. How does Jesus's indignation reveal God's passion for the entire world? What practices and human-originated rituals in the church might serve as barriers between God and vulnerable people in search of God's love?

03 Jesus undoes the status quo of the temple to restore what has been broken. He then restores what is broken (the blind and the lame) to undo the effects of sin and death on humankind. What might Jesus need to undo in our lives—as individuals and as the body of Christ—in order to bring about healing?

PRAYER

Lord, we confess that our imaginations have been shaped by the power practices of this fallen world. Too often, we are more concerned with our habitual way of worship than we are with staying in step with your heart of love for the world. Undo in us the things that have led us away from your heart. Heal us and make us whole, that you might be made known through us.

MONDAY

AM Psalm: 51

PM Psalm: 69:1–23

Jeremiah 12:1–16

John 12:9–19

Philippians 3:1–14

When I was a pastor in rural Missouri, I had the opportunity to watch a Civil War reenactment. Having no knowledge of the culture surrounding these events, I fully anticipated seeing hordes of men dressed in blue Union uniforms and a smattering of gray—a few random individuals who drew the short straw and had to play the role of Confederate because, in my mind, *no one wants to be on the losing side.* Boy, was I wrong. Dozens of men showed up, ready to represent the Confederacy.

I have often wondered the same thing on Palm Sunday: why do we reenact this? We give branches to our children and send them down the sanctuary aisles to shout, "Hosanna! Blessed is he who comes in the name of the Lord!" All the while, with the benefit of hindsight, we know that the crowds' shouts of praise were false. When, mere *days* later, Jesus failed to meet the people's messianic expectations, their praises morphed into shouts of "Crucify him!"

The praise of Palm Sunday only makes sense backwards—when we look back upon Jesus's strange entry into the city from the viewpoint of the empty tomb. Only with hearts illuminated by the Spirit can we see Jesus as the King he truly is: not a political figure of a small nation in the annals of history but the King of creation who will conquer sin and death. As easy as it is to criticize the idolatrous expectations of the crowds, how often do we impose upon God our visions of how God should act?

But, with hearts and minds enlightened by the Spirit, we can wave our palms and shout "Hosanna!" We do not participate in a dead reenactment of an ancient misunderstanding alongside the crowd. With Spirit-illuminated vision we declare, *Hosanna! Save us! Save us from ourselves, from our sin, from our cold, hard hearts. Save us from death, that old enemy that clamors after us. Save us from the lie that we are the measure of righteousness, that our desires are justified simply because we desire them. Save us from our idolatrous expectations and angry disappointment. Save us! Ascend the throne of our hearts and make yourself at home in us.*

God in God's mercy does not give us the king we want—a king of might and power, a king of violence and coercion. Our expectations must die, and not without pain. God does not give us the king we want; but God has given us the King we need. The King we need is the humble man on the donkey, the one who frees us not from political foes but from the chains of sin and death. The King we need does not impose his will with violent force but willingly suffers violence for the sake of love. The King we need is the Prince of Peace, who reconciles us to the Father and to one another.

—*SDL*

REFLECTION & PRACTICE

01 We are again engaging the Palm Sunday account, with crowds shouting praise and palm branches waved in celebration. But we are still only too aware that the week that has begun in joy will reveal a stunning turn of events.

- How do you find yourself caught up in this account? How would you describe the difference between the response of the crowds who have come to see Lazarus and Jesus, and the response of the chief priests?
- What expectations do you think are in the minds of the crowd as they shout praise for Jesus?
- Even the disciples are puzzled at the acclaim the crowds give to Jesus. Why do you think they are not more aware of what is happening?

02 "God does not give us the king we want; but God has given us the King we need." How do you understand that difference in regard to this event? What expectations of ours may need to be set aside in favor of a greater revelation?

03 "The praise of Palm Sunday only makes sense backwards." When have you found it necessary to look backwards in order to see the work of God in your life, in your church, and in our world? How might we gain greater understanding of what God is doing in our own lives as we look backwards?

PRAYER

Father, we are often insistent that you work in the ways we prefer, that we be allowed to live by our own preferences, rather than by the purposes you have for us and for those we love. Teach us to look at life with the long view in mind. Help us to withhold our judgment of your faithfulness long enough that we can grasp something of your perspective rather than demand your conformity with our agenda. Teach us how to praise you, to walk faithfully with you, and to allow you to fulfill your plans for us.

TUESDAY

AM Psalm: 6

PM Psalm: 94

Jeremiah 15:10–21

John 12:20–26

Philippians 3:15–21

The clamoring crowds are still collecting their cloaks from the ground and brushing off the dust. Children still cling tightly to palm branches. But Jesus wastes no time on their idolatrous illusions of salvation. There is no time to carefully tiptoe around sensibilities. The hour has come—to be glorified, yes—but not in the way the crowds imagine.

When I was a child, my classmates and I each tucked a bean deep into a plastic cup of potting soil. Our teacher instructed us to edge the seed toward the transparent side of the cup so we could observe the transformation. We dutifully recorded our daily observations. *Day 1: nothing. Day 2: nothing. Day 5: nothing. Day 6: There's a tiny crack in my seed. I think I need a new one. Day 8: Wait, I don't need a new one. A tiny green string is coming out of my seed! It's alive!*

In a matter of days, Jesus himself will be tucked into the soil, having suffered and died a criminal's death. *We need a new Savior,* the Jews will declare. *This one is broken.* But Jesus knows the truth: death is the gateway to life, not only for himself but also for the world. Through the cracking open, newness can emerge—newness that will propagate and spread.

Jesus's words are testimony but also calling. His self-giving way of being is not only a gift—it is also an invitation. Instead of clinging to this seed-shaped life, we release it in order to experience the life of the age to come, in which we flourish and those around us are nourished. This hard teaching is not framed as add-on for the extreme follower but as a command to *whoever* would serve Jesus. But the promise that follows the command? "Where I am, my servant also will be" (John 12:26). Presence. When planted, we do not enter into the darkness of the soil alone. Jesus enters the darkness with us, into the space where we are broken open by self-giving love. Our obedience does not go unseen by God.

Meanwhile, the two Greeks stand there in silence. This is not the conversation they anticipated having with the man who made such a grand entrance into Jerusalem. It is not a conversation at all. It is, rather, a declaration of a man who is present yet not present, whose eyes seem fixed on something unseen by the rest. Indeed, Jesus's eyes are fixed on the cross—the instrument that will hand him over to the darkness, the soil, in which he will wait.

We too find ourselves present yet not present. We live not toward the triumphs and successes of this life but toward the in-breaking kingdom of God. We are not consumed by what seems so pressing to those around us. We are captivated by the call of our King to a kingdom that breaks in through our broken-open lives as we practice the self-giving love of our Lord.

—*SDL*

REFLECTION & PRACTICE

01 The Greeks ask to see Jesus following the acclaim and excitement of the crowds as Jesus entered Jerusalem. What must have been going through their minds when they heard the words of Jesus? How do you think you would have responded? What do Jesus's words mean to you now?

02 The words of Jesus imply something very different from what the crowds seem to expect. What do these words of testimony by Jesus say about his kingship? To what is Jesus calling his disciples? What is the cost of discipleship?

03 Jesus seems very aware of the price he will pay. What does it mean to you when Jesus says in John 12:25, "Anyone who loves their life will lose it, while anyone who hates their life in this world will keep it for eternal life"? How might the Father honor those who serve Jesus?

PRAYER

Father, we confess that we often desire the benefits and blessings of following you but resist the idea that there may be a cost to us. Help us grasp the depth of your love expressed in the sacrificial love of Jesus on our behalf. May our life in Christ be characterized by a willingness to suffer for the good of others, not for our benefit but for your glory. Teach us how we may participate in the suffering love of Jesus as we live in service to those around us.

WEDNESDAY

AM *Psalm: 55*

PM *Psalm: 74*

Jeremiah 17:5–10, 14–17

John 12:27–36

Philippians 4:1–13

To be human is to be able to have a sense of the future. Unlike the family dog or cat who lives day by day, blissfully unaware of an impending veterinarian appointment, we have full calendars that remind us of everything ahead, good and bad. The impending dread from an upcoming appointment or a painful anniversary weighs on our spirits. Our minds drift from the present moment toward what is to come.

The hour of Christ's distress looms on the horizon. Jesus's attention is drifting from healings, teaching, and confrontations and settling on the travail that is to come. "Now my soul is troubled," he says (John 12:27). Any suggestion that the Jesus of John's Gospel is unfeeling and above the grittiness of the human experience is unmasked as false. Jesus, the Son of Man, is troubled. He is distressed by what the next few days will bring. We could speculate about the source of his troubled spirit: the physical suffering, the feelings of abandonment on the cross, the ugliness of sin that will bare its teeth, the descent into death. Perhaps it is all these things, and more. The source does not change the experience of inner turmoil.

"And what shall I say? 'Father, save me from this hour'?" (v. 27). Unlike the Synoptic Gospels, John does not tell of Jesus weeping and praying in the garden of Gethsemane. Rather, this is the moment in which Jesus asks, *Is this the road I will take? Will I submit myself to becoming the seed that dies in order that all might live? Will I ask the Father to deliver me from the hour of my travail?*

"No, it was for this very reason I came to this hour" (v. 27). Jesus fixes his heart and mind on the hour to come. He sets his gaze on the cross. He will not be deterred, even by the turmoil roiling within him. He faces his desire to prevent the suffering, pain, and the shame to come and bids it submit in obedience to the Father. In the midst of his struggle, Jesus calls out, "Father, glorify your name!" (v. 27). Through Jesus's obedience unto death, the Father will be glorified, and ultimately the name of Jesus will be exalted as well.

In sin-sick creation, desire is the measure of virtue. The mere existence of our longing is ample justification for most behaviors. Our cravings, attractions, and appetites are not merely acknowledged; they are elevated as a source of truth and righteousness. Jesus demonstrates an alternative way of being. Desire is acknowledged but ultimately dethroned, that God might reign in him and through him. As people marked by the cross and enlivened by the Spirit of the resurrection, we too boldly dethrone desire, to the confusion of culture, and allow the triune God to ascend the throne of our hearts.

—*SDL*

REFLECTION & PRACTICE

01 As we draw nearer to the betrayal, arrest, torture, and crucifixion of Jesus, we are sometimes troubled by the humanity of his struggle with what he could see coming. How do you respond to the words of Jesus: "Now my soul is troubled"? What does this imply about his understanding of himself and his understanding of his relationship with the Father? What does it then mean when Jesus prays, "Father, glorify your name!"?

02 The letter to the Hebrews states that Jesus "learned obedience from what he suffered . . ." (5:8). What does it mean to you that Jesus "obeyed" the Father, submitting himself to death on the cross? In what ways is that a pattern for our living for Jesus?

03 "Our cravings, attractions, and appetites are not merely acknowledged; they are elevated as a source of truth and righteousness." How might we dethrone desire as the justification for our living as we choose? What is the resource on which we may rely in order to dethrone our desires?

PRAYER

We come face to face with the inner struggle to genuinely walk in the light, Father. Our desires—even our legitimate desires—can become so enslaving to us that we fail to embrace your call to a higher motive in our living. Teach us how to pattern our lives after the life of your Son. Guide us by your Spirit and teach us through your Word and the fellowship we enjoy with other believers. May our pattern and our motivation be Jesus and his sacrificial love for us.

MAUNDY

THURSDAY

AM Psalm: 102

PM Psalms: 142, 143

Jeremiah 20:7–11

John 17

1 Corinthians 10:14–17; 11:27–32

The hour has come. The Son of Man will be lifted up. While the betrayer gathers his associates, Jesus offers final words of comfort to the remaining eleven. The Gospel of John offers us a unique glimpse into something sacred: the holy intimacy between the Son and the Father. They are one in mission: to give eternal life—the life of the age to come— expressed in relational knowledge of the Father and Son here and now.

As the prayer begins, both the disciples and we, the readers millennia into the future, feel outside the conversation. This is a sacred interaction within the triune Godhead. They are bound together in eternal love, mutual submission, and an enduring mission to redeem creation. But within a few verses, the divine circle opens, and the disciples are brought into the dance. Further in the passage, we—those who believe in Jesus through the message of the disciples—are invited into the circle as well. We are included in the love and fellowship of God.

But our inclusion goes beyond experiencing the joy of divine love; it is also an invitation to join the divine mission. Jesus prays not that his followers will be taken out of the world—the metaphor John uses to represent rebellious, sinful humanity. Rather, he prays that God the Father would protect us *as we are in the world.* He asks that we might be sanctified by the truth of God *as we are sent* into the world. The intent is clear: we are on mission with the triune God to redeem the world.

Jesus goes on to pray for the unity of believers. How often this verse has been cited during a contentious board meeting or church conflict! Yet this verse is less about "getting along" and far more about oneness in mission and purpose. As the Father and Son cooperate in love to redeem the beloved world, so too the church as a reflection of the Trinity cooperates in love to participate in that redemption in the unique contexts into which we have been placed.

Today is Maundy Thursday, the day on which we remember the *mandatum*, or commandment, of Jesus at the Last Supper: "A new command I give you: Love one another. As I have loved you, so you must love one another. By this everyone will know that you are my disciples, if you love one another" (13:34–35). As we seek to live into the holy invitation to join the triune God in mission, this commandment serves as our firm foundation. We begin in love—and not the romanticized teamwork in which everyone always agrees. The love Jesus invites us to pursue is the self-giving love that he himself exemplified. This love heals our sin-sick hearts, restores our faith communities, and gives us the impetus to go out into the world in service.

—*SDL*

REFLECTION & PRACTICE

01 Maundy Thursday draws us deeply into the last hours Jesus spent with his disciples. On that day Jesus poured himself into his disciples, and in the closing prayer we find ourselves listening in on a conversation of deepest intimacy. What do the words of this prayer teach us about the relationship between Jesus and the Father? How do those words impact you? What is the work Jesus has been sent to accomplish?

02 The broadening scope of the prayer of Jesus envelops his disciples. What do we learn about the role of the disciples of Jesus in the fulfillment of his mission? What does Jesus imply about the relationship the disciples will have to the Father? How does that relationship reflect the relationship Jesus has with the Father?

03 The prayer of Jesus is a petition and a promise.
- What does Jesus ask for us—for you and me—in our life in the world?
- What is the nature of the unity for which Jesus prays?
- How is that unity best experienced and expressed?
- How may we experience and demonstrate the intimacy with the Trinity for which Jesus prays?

PRAYER

Father, on this day when the command to love one another is so clearly laid out before us, teach us how to move beyond mere unity. Grip us with the image of your Son, our Savior, laying down his life for our redemption. Help us to grasp the astounding reality that we may participate in the mission of your Son. May the intimacy you have with the Son and the Spirit, as it is expressed in the tangible mission of Jesus, be fulfilled in us. May we bear your love to the world in tangible, practical, and transforming relationships with those around us.

GOOD FRIDAY

AM Psalms: 22, 95

PM Psalms: 40, 54

Genesis 22:1–14

John 13:36–38; 19:38–42

1 Peter 1:10–20

It is finished.

There is nothing more to say. The eleven disciples have scattered. The women remained as witnesses to the atrocities. If watching their Lord suffer the physical anguish was not enough, they were also forced to watch him endure mockery and public humiliation. How could everything have gone so wrong, so quickly?

Nicodemus and Joseph of Arimathea, two men who have been pursuing Jesus in secret, unexpectedly emerge from the shadows. Perhaps they are ashamed of the behavior of their fellow Jewish leaders, or perhaps they are ashamed of their own shadowy discipleship. If only they had spoken up, things might have been different. Their shame and regret are expressed through an act of courage—requesting Jesus's body from Pilate—and through extravagant gifts in the burial spices.

In today's Old Testament reading, Abraham obeys God's command to offer his son Isaac as a sacrifice. In the last moment, God stays Abraham's hand and provides a ram instead. But today there is no ram in the thicket. There is no last-minute reprieve. God does not spare his own Son but gives him up for us all (Romans 8:32).

Jesus's followers have no understanding of the significance of this moment. They are not huddled in back rooms, debating various atonement theories. All they know is that the One in whom they placed their trust is dead. They would be angry if they were not so frightened. They would be overcome by humiliation at their three-year devotion to this seemingly failed Messiah if they were not in fear for their lives.

For those of us today who know that "Sunday's a'comin'," though, we tend to skip over the devastation of this day when death reigned. In some ways, it is impossible not to simply because we *do* know the outcome. But, if we allow ourselves to enter the pain of this moment— when God in Christ has submitted to the powers of sin and death—we may unexpectedly discover solace and even comfort. It is not comfort based on desired outcomes but comfort in the knowledge that we are not alone in our suffering and pain. God does it too. God does not offer us a long-distance remedy for us and for creation—a clean-cut, simple solution to mend what ails us, like some divine round of antibiotics. Rather, God gets low. God enters into the darkest shadows of human experience: abuse, humiliation, shame, violence.

It is Friday. Resist the urge to leap ahead. The cross is still damp with blood. The women have returned to their homes, faces streaked with dust and tears. Joseph of Arimathea and Nicodemus have done all they know to do, and plod home with heavy hearts. The disciples tremble in shadowy back rooms. Each heart echoes the cry that came from Jesus's cracked lips: *"My God, my God, why have you forsaken me?"*

—SDL

REFLECTION & PRACTICE

01 This is the darkest day of the week in the story of Jesus. It is reflection on the events of this day that make a song like "The Old Rugged Cross" resonate with our deepest inner being. Allow yourself to think about the desolation and despair that must have gripped the disciples. What were they feeling? What must Mary, the mother of Jesus, have been experiencing? What were Joseph and Nicodemus experiencing as they labored to remove the body of Jesus from the cross? How does it sink into your own heart?

02 God enters into our own suffering and pain.
- When have you experienced the deepest pain and suffering? How did God manifest God's presence and comfort to you?
- What does it mean to say that God has entered into our suffering?
- How might you walk alongside those who are suffering and in pain?
- Who most needs your assurance that God has not forgotten them? How will you minister a grace of presence that reflects the presence of God?

PRAYER

Father, our hearts wait in silence. Help us avoid the temptation to leap ahead so far that we are unwilling to suffer the reality of your Son's agony and death. May our hearts be struck again by the depth of your love expressed in the death of your Son. May the magnitude of sin and brokenness around us remind us of the reason for the suffering death of Jesus. You have entered into our brokenness and the darkness brought by sin. Help us today to enter with you into your darkness, your grief, in order that we may understand the depth of your love for us.

HOLY SATURDAY

AM Psalms: 88, 95

PM Psalm: 27

Job 19:21–27a

Romans 8:1–11

Hebrews 4:1–16

There is no Gospel reading today. There is only silence. The cross is empty; the tomb is not.

It is finished, Jesus said. The work he came to do is complete. So he rests in a tomb, like a strange parody of the seventh day of the creation account. God is still.

Stillness can feel akin to absence. Is God there? Or are we alone in our sorrow and confusion? Give us a sign, Lord—any indication that we have not been abandoned to the grave.

On that eternal Sabbath, between death and resurrection, all hope is suspended. The day intended to be a gift feels like a jail cell, or perhaps a tomb. No tasks can distract their aching hearts; no work can occupy their restless minds. Jesus's followers can only sit and hold within themselves the grief, the regret, and the fear.

Israel once believed it had entered eternal Sabbath. The promised land would be their home for all time. Because of their disobedience, the generation that was delivered from Egypt would never enter that rest. Yet even the generation that did enter the promised land would discover that there was no everlasting rest to be found as they too abandoned the God of their salvation. There is no rest apart from trusting obedience to God. There is only fearful striving and aching discontent.

In today's passage from Hebrews, the author says, "There remains, then, a Sabbath-rest for the people of God; for anyone who enters God's rest also rests from their works, just as God did from his" (4:9–10). On that bleak Sabbath following the crucifixion, followers of Jesus must have questioned, *how can we rest? How can we be still when Love has died? Is God still? Is God inactive? If so, all hope is lost.*

With God, however, stillness is only the prelude to new creation.

Often we fill the stillness of this day—the holy gap between Good Friday and Easter—with the busyness of community egg hunts, meal preparation, and shopping. We lay out our Sunday best for tomorrow, the lacy socks and tiny button-up shirts. But what if, even if only for a moment, we were still? What if we remembered the stillness of the Sabbath so long ago and placed ourselves in the divine rest of that day? What if we sat in the quiet and remembered: *it is finished*? God has done the work and will bring all things into fullness at just the right time. Can we trust in the stillness? Can we obey in the stillness?

Perhaps, like Job, we might sit, fully present to the sorrow of this day but still lifting our eyes in hope that divine silence is not divine absence. With hope, we watch the sky and whisper, *I know that my Redeemer lives and that in the end he will stand on the earth.*

—*SDL*

REFLECTION & PRACTICE

01 This was a bleak Sabbath for the followers of Jesus. All their hopes and dreams came crashing down with the deepening darkness, and the now sealed tomb.

- Have you experienced a period of utter darkness, of silence, when there seemed to be no way forward? How did you navigate the experience?
- When God is silent, is God also inactive? What could be the purpose of that long, silent day?

02 We are prone to fill silence with busyness and talk. How might we more appropriately engage in the significance of the silence of this day? What lessons might we learn from this silence? How may it become a means of Sabbath rest?

03 "With God, stillness is only the prelude to new creation."

- How is our waiting informed by the life, ministry, and teachings of Jesus?
- What has Jesus taught us about the purposes and the character of God?
- How does that prepare us for this bleak Sabbath?

PRAYER

Father, we prefer singing over silence. We prefer busyness over waiting. Teach us, especially today, how to wait before you in careful evaluation, in a searching of our hearts, in order that we may prepare ourselves for when you will speak. May our understanding of the meaning of this long, quiet day begin to stir in us an anticipation that, though you are silent, you are not inactive. Prepare us for your new creation!

EASTER SUNDAY

AM Psalms: 148, 149, 150

PM Psalms: 113, 114

Exodus 12:1–14

Isaiah 51:9–11

John 1:1–18; 20:19–23

Alleluia!

The long night has passed, and dawn has broken on the horizon. The curse of sin and death that has bound up creation for so long has been undone. Our healing has begun!

On the evening of the resurrection the disciples gather together, still consumed by anxiety and lack of understanding. Even as they hide in fear, Jesus comes to them. He comes not to belittle their ignorance or shame them for their betrayal. Rather, he comes to breathe peace.

The Gospel of John begins not with John the Baptist or the birth narrative of Jesus but with the story of creation. Through the pre-incarnate Christ, all things came into being. The triune God formed humankind from the dust of the earth and breathed into them the breath of life. The breath of God creates, awakens, and enlivens.

In Exodus, when the people of God are trapped between the sea and the armies of Pharaoh, God unleashes the divine breath again: "By the blast of your nostrils the waters piled up" (15:8). When the chariots of the enemy encroach the fleeing people, Miriam declares, "You blew with your breath, and the sea covered them" (v. 10). Salvation and new life are once again breathed into the people of God from God's very self.

In Ezekiel, the prophet is commanded to prophesy to the breath and cry out, "Come, breath, from the four winds and breathe into these slain, that they may live" (37:9). Divine breath comes and enlivens a whole valley of the slain.

When the resurrected Christ breathes upon the disciples, we hear not a singular exhale but a whole history of the divine breath being unleashed upon the people of God. Jesus exhales the creating, delivering, resurrecting Spirit upon his followers. By the breath, they are re-created into the faithful people of God and are thus commissioned to participate in the divine work of redemption as agents of reconciliation.

The same Spirit that Christ breathed upon the disciples has fallen now upon us, the church. We too are being shaped into a faithful people. We are being re-created in the image of Christlikeness. We are invited to embrace our vocation as kingdom people, agents of divine reconciliation. The resurrecting Spirit of Christ strengthens and empowers us, heals and restores us.

Empowered by the breath of God, let us declare the mystery of our faith: Christ has died; Christ is risen; Christ will come again.

Alleluia!

—SDL

REFLECTION & PRACTICE

01 Around the globe today, Christian believers are shouting, singing—
and in some cases by necessity, whispering—this reality: "Christ is
risen!" And in response other believers are answering in great joy, "He
is risen, indeed!" This morning, allow yourself to lean into that joyous
reality. How will you allow this reality to shape how you think, live,
and relate to others today and in the days to come? What circumstance
in your life or in the life of a friend or loved one may be transformed
by the resurrection of Jesus?

02 The ancient people of God looked forward to "the day of the Lord" and
the beginning of the "age to come." For the Christian, the resurrection
of Jesus was that day, and the new creation has begun. It is not yet
brought into finality, but even now, we are living in the "age to come."
How might this reality shape our perception of what God is doing in
our world today? How is the breath of the Spirit at work in your life?
Where do you see the old passed away and new creation reshaping
you? How are you becoming an agent of divine reconciliation?

PRAYER

*Glorious Father, we are breathless with joy as we celebrate the resurrection of
Jesus Christ with your people around the world. May our celebration move
us away from easy familiarity with the story of that first Easter. Somehow,
may the stunning reality of the resurrection disturb our complacency and
awaken us to the wonder and joy that fill this day. Help us to see the utter
disruption of the reign of sin and brokenness that has been accomplished. We
sing our praise to one another: "He is risen!" And all creation responds with
our brothers and sisters, "He is risen, indeed!" Amen.*

ABOUT

THE AUTHORS

DR. JESSE C MIDDENDORF is executive director of the Center for Pastoral Leadership at Nazarene Theological Seminary. He served for twenty-eight years as a pastor in the Church of the Nazarene, five years as a district superintendent, and twelve years as a general superintendent, retiring in 2013. He and his wife, Susan, have been married for more than fifty-five years and have three children and seven grandchildren.

REV. STEPHANIE DYRNESS LOBDELL, MDiv, is a pastor and writer. She served as co-lead pastor with her husband, Tommy, for ten years in the Church of the Nazarene and is now the campus pastor at Mount Vernon Nazarene University in Ohio. She is the author of *Signs of Life: Resurrecting Hope out of Ordinary Losses*. Stephanie and Tommy have two children, Josephine and Jack.